STECK-VAUGHN

Vocabulary Advantage

FOR

Science

Student Work Text

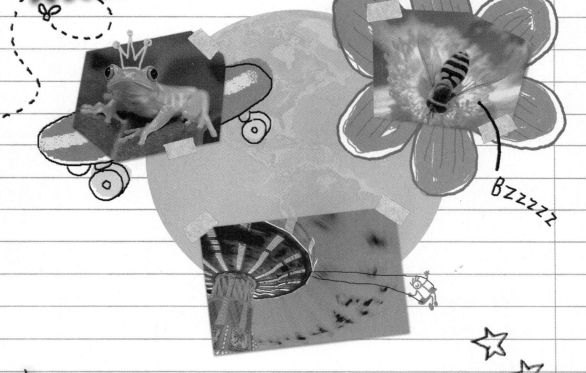

Bzzzzz

Vivian Bernstein

Steck Vaughn™

A Harcourt Achieve Imprint

www.Steck-Vaughn.com
1-800-531-5015

Acknowledgements

Executive Editor	Eduardo Aparicio
Senior Editor	Victoria Davis
Design Team	Cindi Ellis, Cynthia Hannon, Jean O'Dette
Media Researchers	Nicole Mlakar, Stephanie Arsenault
Production Team	Mychael Ferris-Pacheco, Paula Schumann, Alia Hasan
Creative Team	Joan Cunningham, Alan Klemp

Photo Credits

Page 20 ©Jim Zipp/Photo Researchers, Inc.; p. 32 ©George Harrison/ Grant Heilman Photography; p. 38 ©Bettmann/CORBIS; p. 50 ©Gianni Dagli Orti/CORBIS; p. 74 ©Granger Collection, NY; p. 82 ©Hashimoto Noboru/CORBIS SYGMA.

Additional photography by Artville/Getty Images Royalty Free, Brand X Images/Getty Images Royalty Free, Comstock Royalty Free, Digital Vision/Getty Images Royalty Free, PhotoDisc/Getty Images Royalty Free, Photos.com Royalty Free, Royalty-Free/CORBIS, Sam Dudgeon/HRW Photo, Stockbyte Royalty Free.

ISBN 1-4190-1889-2

© 2007 Harcourt Achieve Inc.

All rights reserved. No part of the material protected by this copyright may be reproduced or utilized in any form or by any means, in whole or in part, without permission in writing from the copyright owner. Requests for permission should be mailed to: Paralegal Department, 6277 Sea Harbor Drive, Orlando, FL 32887

Steck-Vaughn is a trademark of Harcourt Achieve Inc.

Printed in the United States of America
1 2 3 4 5 6 7 8 082 12 11 10 09 08 07 06 05

Dear Student,

Welcome to *Vocabulary Advantage for Science*!

In this Student Work Text, you will

- learn new science words that will help you better understand what you read in your science textbook,

- learn useful words that will help you in the classroom and on tests,

- and learn skills that will help you figure out the meaning of other new words you meet.

You will write and talk—a lot!—about the new words you've learned. You should also feel free to draw, circle, underline, and make notes on the pages of this Work Text to help you remember what the new words mean. You can do more writing and drawing in your Science Vocabulary Journal.

All of the tools in this book will help you build your own understanding of important science and classroom vocabulary. Building your understanding of these words will give you an advantage in your science class and on science tests!

Have fun!

Table of Contents

Read the passage below. Think about the meanings of the new words printed in **bold**. Underline any definitions that might help you figure out what these words mean. The first one has been done for you.

Who Writes This Stuff?

Vocabulary Strategy

Writers will often place definitions of new or difficult words near those words in text. Look for these definitions in the text to help you understand new words you find.

Your science textbook tells about plants, animals, the earth, and space. Did you ever wonder about the person who wrote your book?

The author of your textbook is probably a **scientist**. <u>A scientist is someone who is an expert in science.</u> The author decides what things to teach in the book. The author might decide to teach the **law** of motion, for example. This law is a rule that explains why objects always move in a certain way. The author also chooses which **theories** to include. A theory is a statement based on facts.

After the book is written, the author might decide to add photographs, drawings, and **charts**. A chart is a drawing that shows information in a way that is easy to understand.

It takes a lot of work to write a textbook. It might be even harder to learn without one, however!

New Science Words

chart
noun a drawing that shows information in a way that makes it easy to understand

law
noun a rule that says that things should always happen in a certain way

scientist
noun a person who is an expert in science

theory
noun a statement, based on facts, that explains why or how something happens

Now read this passage and practice the vocabulary strategy again. Underline any definitions in the passage that help you figure out what the new words in **bold** mean.

Using the Scientific Method

The scientific method is a special way of testing ideas. In the first step you observe, or watch, something and ask questions about it. Then, you come up with a **hypothesis**. This is your guess about what you saw. The next step is to test your hypothesis by doing an **experiment**. An experiment is a test to find out if your hypothesis is correct.

You might use a **control** in your experiment. The **results** from the experiment, or what you discover, should be compared to the control. You may put your results in a **graph**, a drawing that helps you compare numbers.

Another kind of experiment might use a **model**. You use a model to show what you observed.

"As the **graph** shows, my subject fell asleep during the **experiment**."

 More New Science Words

control

noun   something in an experiment that everything else is compared to

verb   to have power over something

experiment

noun   a scientific test that is done to prove something or to find how one thing affects another

graph

noun   a kind of drawing that compares numbers or amounts using lines, bars, or parts of a circle

model

noun   a copy of something that shows its details, how it works, or what it is made of

 Other Useful Words

hypothesis

noun   a guess or an idea that can be tested

results

noun   what is discovered or learned from an experiment

Use the Strategy

Look at a chapter in your science textbook that your teacher identifies. Use definitions in the text to help you figure out the meanings of any new words you find.

Find the Word

Write a word from the box next to each clue. Then write the word made by the boxed letters. It tells you something you might find in a dream.

graph	model	control	law	hypothesis
experiment	chart	theory	scientist	

1. results are compared to this __ __ ☐ __ __ __ __

2. a test of an idea __ __ __ __ ☐ __ __ __ __

3. a drawing that compares numbers ☐ __ __ __ __

4. an idea or guess __ __ __ __ ☐ __ __ __ __

5. a statement that explains ☐ __ __ __ __ __

6. a copy of something ☐ __ __ __ __

7. a rule __ ☐ __

8. a drawing that shows information __ __ __ ☐ __

9. a science expert __ __ __ ☐ __ __ __ __ __

Answer: __ __ __ __ __ __

Word Challenge: Correct or Incorrect

Take turns with a partner reading the sentences below out loud. Write **C** if the sentence is correct, and write **I** if the sentence is incorrect. Rewrite the incorrect sentences. The first one has been done for you.

1 __C__ The **scientist** studied the way birds build their nests.

2 _____ Anya made a **hypothesis** to show how much her dog has grown.

_____

3 _____ Liam drew a **graph** to compare the prices of new bicycles.

_____

4 _____ Mateo wants to do an **experiment** to prove that he likes pizza.

_____

Word Challenge: Which Word ?

With a partner, take turns saying the words listed below. Together, think of a statement for each one that gives a clue about its meaning. Write your statement next to the word. The first one has been done for you.

1 **experiment** _"I put ideas to the test."_____

2 **control** _____

3 **theory** _____

4 **results** _____

5

Extend the Meaning

Write the letter of the word or phrase that best completes each sentence. Discuss your answers with a partner.

1 A **theory** might _____.
   a. show how to do an experiment
   b. explain why flowers are certain colors
   c. tell the number of people living in a city

2 A **graph** might show _____.
   a. the amount of rainfall for each month of a year
   b. a drawing of a leaf
   c. the state capital

3 You might do an **experiment** to _____.
   a. find out what weeks have the sunniest days
   b. draw a map
   c. read a book before watching TV

4 A **law** might _____.
   a. show different places on a map
   b. explain why things fall to the ground
   c. compare two ideas to find out which one is better

Word Study: The -ing Ending

When the -ing ending is added to a noun such as *chart*, it does two things:
- First, it makes the noun a verb: *charting*.
- Second, it changes the word's meaning. The word now means "to make a chart."

chart (n.) a drawing that shows information in a way that makes it easy to understand
charting (v.) to make a drawing that shows information

Add -ing to the words below. Write definitions for the new words you made. Use a dictionary to check your spelling and definitions.

	+ -ing	Meaning
1 experiment		
2 graph		
3 model		
4 control		

The Language of Testing

How would you answer a question like this on a test?

All of the following statements are true (except)

A. An experiment is a kind of test to prove something is true or false.
B. A scientist might study how light and water affect plant growth.
C. A theory and a hypothesis are the same.
D. A graph is one kind of chart.

 Tip

The word *except* means you should look for something that means the opposite of the word or phrase before *except*. The opposite of true is false. So in this question, you should look for the answer that is false.

Test Strategy: Read the question carefully so you are sure you understand it. Then, if it has the word *except* in it, ask the question in a different way. Remember that you are looking for the statement that is false.

1 How could you say the question above in a different way?

_____

_____

Try the strategy again by asking these questions in a different way.

2 Each of the following things is a type of chart except

A. graph
B. diagram
C. table
D. model

3 All of the following statements are false except

A. A graph is not a kind of chart.
B. Scientists know about science.
C. A model is also a theory.
D. A law is rarely followed.

_____   _____

_____   _____

_____   _____

In Your Vocabulary Journal

Find each of these words in your Science Vocabulary Journal. Working by yourself or with a partner, use the definitions from pages 2 and 3 of your Work Text to complete the rest of the entry for each word.

chart	control	experiment	graph	hypothesis
law	model	results	scientist	theory

Lesson 2 Living Things

Read the passage below. Think about the meanings of the words printed in **bold**. Create connections between words you know and the new words. These will help you remember what the new words mean. Write these connections near the new words in the passage. The first one has been done for you.

 The Scoop on Cells

building blocks

Vocabulary Strategy

Create connections between things you know and new words to "anchor" your understanding of new words. You can use a Word Anchor chart to help you create connections.

What's the big deal about **cells**? Cells are living building blocks. All living things are made of cells. Some plants and animals only have one cell. Others have millions and millions of cells. Scientists believe the human body has more than 10 trillion cells. That's 10,000,000,000,000 cells!

We can **classify**, or group, cells in many ways. For example, there are plant cells and animal cells. We can also classify cells by where they are in the body. There are nerve, bone, skin, and muscle cells.

The center of the cell is the **nucleus**. It's like the cell's brain. It holds all of the information about the plant or animal that the cell belongs to. If you could read the information in the nucleus, you would know the **species**, or special kind of plant or animal that the cell comes from.

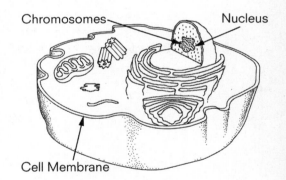

Chromosomes

Nucleus

Cell Membrane

Animal Cell

 New Science Words

cell
   noun the smallest part of all living things

classify
   verb to sort things into groups by how they are alike

nucleus
   noun the central part of a cell

species
   noun a group of plants or animals that are alike in important ways

Now read this passage and practice the vocabulary strategy again. Write near the new words or mark in the passage any connections that will help you "anchor" the meaning of the new words.

It Can Make You Sick!

Bacteria are among the smallest of all living things. They are **simple** creatures, made of a single cell. Some bacteria are helpful. Other bacteria can cause sickness and disease.

A person becomes sick when certain kinds of bacteria **reproduce**. The bacteria **divide** or split to make copies of themselves. Sometimes these bacteria reproduce very quickly. They can **form** or make a large army of bacteria in no time at all. Bacteria give off a poison that the body cannot fight. When this happens, people take medicines to kill the bacteria. Some bacteria have started to **adapt** to the medicines, however. The bacteria change so that the medicine no longer works.

You have millions of different bacteria living on or in your body. The best way to protect yourself from sickness is to wash your hands often.

More New Science Words

adapt

   verb   to change to fit into a new or different situation

bacteria

   noun   very tiny living things that can either be helpful or cause disease

reproduce

   verb   to make a copy of something or to produce young

simple

   adjective   having few parts or details

Other Useful Words

divide

   verb   to split into two or more parts

form

   verb   to make something

"I hate it when she does that!"

Use the Strategy

Look at a chapter in your science textbook that your teacher identifies. Use connections to help you anchor the meaning of any new words you find.

Finish the Sentence

Use a word from the box to finish each sentence. Write the correct word on the line. Discuss your choices with a partner.

adapt	cells	reproduce	simple

1. Some animals _____ to living in the snow by growing white fur.

2. When animals _____, they have babies.

3. The teacher told us that bacteria were _____ one-celled animals.

4. Every living thing is made of _____.

classified	divide	form	nucleus

5. After the field trip, we _____ the different shells we had collected by their size and shape.

6. The _____ controls all of the actions of a cell.

7. Our teacher asked us to _____ a line to go into the museum.

8. We had to _____ the two cookies so all four of us could have some.

Word Challenge: Finish the Idea

With a partner, take turns reading the incomplete sentences below. Write an ending for each. The first one has been done for you.

1 Bears and deer are different **species** because _they are different from one another._

2 Some people think all **bacteria** are bad because _____
_____

3 A **nucleus** is important because _____
_____

4 **Cells** are called the building blocks of life because _____
_____

Word Challenge: What's Your Answer?

Take turns with a partner reading each question out loud and writing an answer on the line. Answer the questions in complete sentences. The first one has been done for you.

1 Where could you find the **nucleus** of a cell? _The nucleus is usually_
in the center of the cell.

2 Why might an animal have to **adapt**? _____
_____

3 What is a **simple** plant? _____
_____

4 How do bacteria **form** copies of themselves? _____
_____

Write the letter of the word or phrase that best completes the sentence. Discuss your choices with a partner.

1 For our science project, we had to _____ each of the animals by its species.

  a. **bacteria**   b. **nucleus**   c. **reproduce**   d. **classify**

2 The medicine didn't work because the bacteria had _____ to it.

  a. **nucleus**   b. **classified**   c. **adapted**   d. **simple**

3 _____ or one-celled plants can reproduce and make new plants in just a few weeks.

  a. **Simple**   b. **Species**   c. **Divided**   d. **Classified**

4 The _____ is part of a cell and is usually seen near the center.

  a. **bacteria**   b. **nucleus**   c. **species**   d. **form**

Word Study: The Prefix re-

The prefix re- means "to do something again." When it is added to a verb such as *divide*, it changes the verb's meaning. The verb now means "to divide again."

> **divide** (v.) to split into two or more parts
> **redivide** (v.) to split into two or more parts again

A. Add re- to the following words.

	+ re-
1 form	
2 classify	
3 produce	

B. Fill in each blank with an re- word from the chart above.

1 Chickens _____ by laying eggs.

2 If a plan you form doesn't work, you will need to _____ it.

The Language of Testing

How would you answer a question like this on a test?

Which of the following explains the word *cell*?

    A. a way of sorting things that are alike
    B. plants or animals that are alike
    C. the smallest part of all living things
    D. basic and easy to understand

 Tip

The phrase *which of the following* means that you have to choose one of the answers listed (A, B, C, or D) to answer the question.

Test Strategy: If the question has the phrase *which of the following* in it, ask the question in a different way. Start your restated question with *what*, *who*, or *where*.

1 How could you say the question above in a different way?

_____

_____

Try the strategy again by asking these questions in a different way.

2 Which of the following explains the meaning of *adapt*?

    A. to change
    B. to sort things that are alike into groups
    C. to copy or to produce young
    D. to make better

_____

_____

_____

3 Which of the following is the definition of *species*?

    A. the central part of a cell
    B. the smallest part of a living thing
    C. sorting things into groups
    D. a group of plants or animals that are alike in certain ways

_____

_____

_____

In Your Vocabulary Journal

Find each of these words in your Science Vocabulary Journal. Working by yourself or with a partner, use the definitions from pages 8 and 9 of your Work Text to complete the rest of the entry for each word.

adapt	**bacteria**	**cell**	**classify**	**divide**
form	**nucleus**	**reproduce**	**simple**	**species**

Plants and Funguses

Read the passage below. Think about the meanings of the new words printed in **bold**. Underline any examples or descriptions you find that might help you figure out the meaning of these words. The first one has been done for you.

Getting Ready for Spring

Vocabulary Strategy

Sometimes writers give examples and descriptions to explain hard words and ideas. Look for clues, like *example*, *like*, or *such as*. Look for pictures that show what a new word means, too.

Many people who have gardens plant seeds in winter. They plant them in pots that they keep inside by a window. The seeds soon begin to **sprout** and grow. With enough light and water, the **sprouts** grow out of the seed and up through the dirt. <u>These sprouts look like thin green threads.</u> As the sprouts grow, they become **seedlings**. These young plants are tiny, but they usually have a **leaf** or two.

Photosynthesis happens inside the green leaves. Just like food is turned into energy in our bodies, photosynthesis turns water, air, and light into energy for the plant.

With care, the seedlings will grow into young plants. They can be moved outside when spring comes. The tiny sprouts from seeds will soon turn into a garden of flowers and vegetables.

New Science Words

leaf
noun   part of a plant that is flat, thin, and usually green

photosynthesis
noun   how green plants make food from sunlight, water, and air

seedling
noun   a young plant that has its first leaves

sprout
verb   to grow from a seed
noun   a very young plant just coming out of its seed

Now read this passage and practice the vocabulary strategy again. Underline the examples and descriptions in the passage. Draw an arrow from each to the word it describes.

Good Fungus – Bad Fungus

How about some **fungus** with your burger? Sounds gross, huh? But mushrooms are fungus. Many people enjoy eating mushrooms on burgers and steaks.

Unlike green plants, a fungus does not make its own food. Often, a fungus feeds on dead plants, a fallen tree, or leaves on the ground. The fungus breaks down the dead plants like a food chopper breaks up food. The tiny bits of dead plant material help make the soil rich.

Along with the good things funguses do, there are also some bad things. Wild mushrooms have poison in them. Another fungus grows under the ground on the **root** of the soybean plant. It grows like mold grows on bread. This fungus can kill the whole plant. Another fungus called "**stem** rust" attacks **grain**, such as wheat. This fungus grows onto a plant's stem, or the part of the plant that stands up out of the ground.

"We have some tasty **roots** tonight, sir."

More New Science Words

fungus
  noun a living thing that is like a plant but has no roots, leaves, or flowers

grain
  noun a small, hard seed that is often eaten for food or a small piece of something, like sand

root
  noun the part of a plant that grows under the ground

stem
  noun the thin, upright part of a plant above ground

Other Useful Words

compare
  verb to look at two things to see how they are alike and different

notice
  verb to see or to become aware of something

Use the Strategy

Look at a chapter in your science textbook that your teacher identifies. Use examples, descriptions, and pictures in the text to help you figure out the meaning of any new words you find. You may want to draw pictures to help you remember what the new words mean.

Matching

Finish the sentences in Group A with words from Group B. Write the letter of the word on the line. Discuss your choices with a partner.

Group A

1. The tall, thin _____ of the plant had several leaves growing on it.

2. The sunlight and air helped the grass carry out _____.

3. We moved the young _____ from the flower pot to the garden.

4. We watered the seeds, and soon they began to _____.

Group B

A. seedling
B. photosynthesis
C. stem
D. sprout

Group A

5. To get rid of the weed, we had to dig its _____ out of the ground.

6. The shape of the _____ told us it had fallen from an oak tree.

7. Rick likes to _____ prices before he buys anything.

8. When we passed the store, did you _____ if it was open?

Group B

E. roots
F. compare
G. leaf
H. notice

Word Challenge: True or False

Take turns with a partner reading the sentences below out loud. Write **T** next to each sentence that is true. Write **F** next to each sentence that is false. Rewrite the sentences that are false. The first one has been done for you.

1 _F_ **Sprouts** grow underground.

Sprouts grow on top of the ground.

2 ____ The **root** is part of a plant that is flat, thin, and green.

_____

3 ____ People eat **grains** such as wheat, corn, and oats in cereal.

_____

4 ____ Plants make sunlight with **photosynthesis**.

_____

Word Challenge: Which Word?

With a partner, take turns saying the words listed below. Together, think of a statement for each one that gives a strong clue about its meaning. Write your statement next to the word. The first one has been done for you.

1 fungus _"I eat dead leaves."_

2 root _____

3 sprout _____

4 seedling _____

Finish the Idea

Finish each idea to make a complete sentence. Write your answer on the line. Discuss your answers with a partner.

1. I might look for a **fungus** in the forest because _____

_____.

2. I would **notice** a dog riding a motorcycle because _____

_____.

3. I would **compare** two different leaves by _____

_____.

4. I could make a seed **sprout** by _____

_____.

Word Study: The Suffix *-less*

When the suffix *–less* is added to a noun such as *stem*, it changes the word's meaning.
- First, it makes the noun an adjective: *stemless*.
- Second, it adds *without* to the meaning of the word.

stem (n.) the thin upright part of a plant
stemless (adj.) without a stem

A. Add *-less* to the following words. Then write a definition for each new word.

	+ *-less*	Meaning
1. leaf		
2. root		
3. seed		

B. Fill in each blank with a *-less* word from the chart above.

1. In fall, leaves fall from the trees. In winter, the trees are _____.

2. I like to eat grapes that do not have seeds. I like _____ grapes.

3. When a seed is planted, it doesn't have roots. It is _____.

18

The Language of Testing

How would you answer a question like this on a test?

What is a **characteristic** of a fungus?

    A. It has roots.
    B. It has flowers.
    C. It grows in damp places.
    D. It makes food through photosynthesis.

 Tip

A *characteristic* of a thing is something that it usually has or does.

Test Strategy: If you see a question that uses the word characteristic, rewrite it to ask for something that is true about the subject of the question.

1 How could you say the question above in a different way?

_____

_____

Try the strategy again by asking these questions in a different way.

2 What is a characteristic of plants that use photosynthesis to make food?

    A. They grow in dark, damp places.
    B. They have green leaves.
    C. They always grow in forests.
    D. They are a type of fungus.

_____

_____

_____

3 What is a characteristic of seedlings?

    A. They have a long stem.
    B. They have long roots.
    C. They are still attached to a seed.
    D. They give off spores.

_____

_____

_____

In Your Vocabulary Journal

Find each of these words in your Science Vocabulary Journal. Working by yourself or with a partner, use the definitions from pages 14 and 15 of your Work Text to complete the rest of the entry for each word.

compare	**fungus**	**grain**	**leaf**	**notice**
photosynthesis	**root**	**seedling**	**sprout**	**stem**

Read the passage below. Think about the meanings of the new words printed in **bold**. Underline any words or phrases that contrast a word you know with a new word or idea. The first one has been done for you.

It's a Frog's Life

Vocabulary Strategy

Use contrasts to help you understand the meanings of new words. Look for clues that point out contrasts such as *unlike*, *instead*, or *different from*.

A frog's life begins when a female frog makes eggs in her **ovaries**. Tiny frog **embryos** are inside the egg. The embryos grow into tadpoles inside the eggs. The tadpoles **hatch** from the eggs underwater. Unlike adult frogs, tadpoles have tails. Soon the tadpoles **develop**, or grow legs and begin to breathe air. The tadpoles are now frogs. They move out of the water onto the land.

Frogs are **amphibians**. Amphibians live in water when they are young and on land when they've grown. They are different from lizards and toads, which live on land their whole life.

Frogs live all over the world. In some dry places, frogs bury themselves deep in the ground. When it rains, all these frogs come up to the surface. It looks like it's been raining frogs!

New Science Words

amphibian
noun   a cold-blooded animal that lives in water when it is young and on land when it is older

embryo
noun   an early part of an animal's life, not long before it is born

hatch
verb   to come out of an egg

ovary
noun   the part of a female animal's body that makes eggs

Now read this passage and practice the vocabulary strategy again. Underline any words or phrases that contrast something you know with a new word or idea. Look for clues like *unlike*, *instead*, or *different from*.

You're Getting Warmer

If you've ever held a lizard or a snake, you know that they aren't very warm. Lizards and snakes are **reptiles**. Reptiles are cold-blooded. Their bodies don't make their own heat so they need to warm themselves in the sun. Reptiles also are not furry like a rabbit. Instead, their bodies are often covered with scales.

Unlike reptiles, **mammals** such as rabbits are warm-blooded. Their bodies make heat. Also, instead of scales, most mammals have hair or fur. However, both reptiles and mammals are **vertebrates**. They have backbones, unlike some animals such as jellyfish.

The largest reptile that ever lived was the **dinosaur**. The largest *living* mammal scientists can **identify** is the blue whale. It can grow to be 100 feet long!

More New Science Words

dinosaur
noun   a large animal that lived many thousands of years ago

mammal
noun   a kind of warm-blooded animal that feeds its babies milk

reptile
noun   a kind of cold-blooded animal that lays eggs and is often covered with scales

vertebrate
noun   a kind of animal that has a backbone

Other Useful Words

develop
verb   to grow or change over a period of time

identify
verb   to name or point out a certain person, animal, or thing

Use the Strategy

Look at a chapter in your textbook that your teacher identifies. Use contrasts to help you figure out the meaning of any new words you find. Keep track of these contrasts in a chart.

Finish the Paragraph

Use the words in bold to finish the paragraph below. Write the words in the blanks. One word will not be used.

amphibians   **hatch**   **reptile**

dinosaur   **mammals**   **vertebrate**

Ms. Gonzales took her class on a field trip to the zoo. The first kind of animals

they saw were the _____ , which included frogs, toads, and
                          1

salamanders. Next, the tour of the giant bird cage was really interesting. The class got

to see parrots and peacocks. As they left the cage, the class watched a baby robin

_____ from its egg. There were a lot of different snakes
          2

in the _____ house. One snake from South America was
          3

almost 20 feet long! The class had lunch near the area of the zoo where the

_____ lived. While they ate, they watched bears, elephants, and
          4

leopards. Later, as they were leaving the zoo, the class saw gigantic bones from a

_____ that roamed the earth millions of years ago.
          5

Word Challenge: Correct or Incorrect

Take turns with a partner reading the sentences below out loud. Write **C** if the sentence is correct, and write **I** if the sentence is incorrect. Rewrite the incorrect sentences. The first one has been done for you.

1   _I_   Many **vertebrates** have shells because they do not have backbones.

     Vertebrates have backbones. _____

2   _____   **Reptiles** can keep their bodies warm.

     _____

3   _____   Both male and female animals have **ovaries**.

     _____

4   _____   An **amphibian** can live both in water and on land.

     _____

Word Challenge: Example/Not an Example

With a partner or by yourself, think of things that are and are not examples of the words listed below. Write your responses in the chart. The first one has been done for you.

		Example	Not an Example
1	dinosour	A Tyrannosaurus rex that lived a long time ago	A lizard in my yard
2	develop		
3	identity		
4	hatch		

Analogies

Use a word from the box to finish each sentence. Write the word on the line. Discuss your answers with a partner.

amphibian	dinosaur	embryo	reptile

1. Snake is to _____ as robin is to bird.

2. Frog is to _____ as cow is to mammal.

3. Animal is to _____ as plant is to seed.

4. Long ago is to _____ as today is to you.

Word Study: The Suffix -ian

When the suffix -ian is added to a noun such as *mammal*, it does two things:
- First, it makes the noun an adjective: *mammalian*.
- Second, the word now describes something that belongs to a mammal.

Drop the -y or -e from the end of a word before adding -ian.

A. Add -ian to each root noun to make a new word. Use a dictionary to check your spelling.

	+ -ian
1. **mammal**	
2. **ovary**	
3. **reptile**	

B. Complete each definition by writing the correct -ian word in the blank. You may use a dictionary to check your answers.

1. _____ *adjective* describes something belonging to mammals.

2. _____ *adjective* describes something belonging to reptiles.

24

The Language of Testing

How would you answer a question like this on a test?

Identify which animal is an amphibian.

- A. bird
- B. frog
- C. horse
- D. snake

Tip

The word *identify* means to point out or name. In a test question, it means that you need to choose or pick the correct answer.

Test Strategy: If you see a question that uses the word *identify*, rewrite it using the words *choose* or *pick*.

1 How could you say the question above a different way?

_____

_____

Try the strategy again by asking these questions in a different way.

2 Identify the correct definition of *ovary*.

- A. the body part of a female animal that makes eggs
- B. a cold-blooded reptile
- C. a type of embryo
- D. a place where birds live

3 Identify the warm-blooded animal.

- A. fish
- B. lizard
- C. dog
- D. salamander

_____   _____

_____   _____

_____   _____

In Your Vocabulary Journal

Find each of these words in your Science Vocabulary Journal. Working by yourself or with a partner, use the definitions from pages 20 and 21 of your Work Text to complete the rest of the entry for each word.

amphibian	develop	dinosaur	embryo	hatch
identify	mammal	ovary	reptile	vertebrate

Lesson 5 The Food Web

Read the passage below. Think about the meanings of the new words printed in **bold**. Circle any any synonyms, or words that mean the same as the new words. Draw an arrow from each synonym to the new word it describes. The first one has been done for you.

In the Rain Forest

Vocabulary Strategy

Use synonyms, or words that mean about the same as the new words to help you understand their meaning. Look for clues like the word *or* to help you find synonyms in a text.

The rain forests of South America hold thousands of species of plants and animals. There is a **relationship** among all of these living things in the rain forest. This relationship, or connection, makes the rain forest an interesting place to study. Every plant and animal has a special purpose, or **role**, in the food web of the rain forest.

The food web is like a big circle, or **cycle**. This cycle begins when the sun **produces**, or makes, light so that plants can grow. Sunlight provides **energy** for the plants. They draw strength from the sunlight. Animals get energy by eating the plants. Other animals get energy by eating these animals. When the plants and animals die, they rot and go back to the soil. Plants grow in the soil, finishing the cycle.

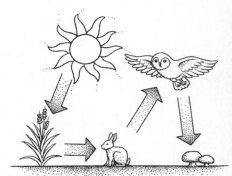

New Science Words

cycle

noun a string of things that happen over and over again in the same order

energy

noun the power or strength needed to do work or grow

produce

verb to make something or to make something happen

relationship

noun how one thing connects to or affects another

role

noun the job that someone or something has to do

Now read this passage and practice the vocabulary strategy again. Circle any synonyms and draw an arrow from each one to the new word it describes.

How to Make Compost

Many gardeners like to make compost. Compost is a mixture of dead plants and dirt. When dead plants break down they put **nutrients** back into the soil. Compost nutrients are a kind of plant food. Just like we eat food, plants **consume** or take in the nutrients in compost. Gardeners put compost in the flowerbeds and vegetable gardens to make the plants grow.

Compost is easy to make. All you need is some dead plant material. For **example**, fruits and vegetables are good for making **compost**. Place these items, or some grass and leaves, in a pile. Add a layer of dirt. Over time, keep adding plants and dirt in layers. When these things **decay**, or rot, they produce compost. Let the pile sit for six to seven months. Waiting this long will **cause** the compost to become richer. After a while, you'll have a fresh batch of compost!

"**Consume** faster! We need more **compost**!"

More New Science Words

consume
  verb   to eat, take in, or use up
decay
  verb   to rot or break down
nutrients
  noun   something that plants and animals
          need to stay strong and healthy

Other Useful Words

cause
  verb   to make something happen
  noun   the reason why something happens
example
  noun   something that can stand for a certain group

Use the Strategy

Look at a chapter in your science textbook that your teacher identifies. Use synonyms in the text to help you understand the meaning of any new words you find. Keep track of new words and their synonyms in a chart.

Find the Word

Write a word from the box next to each clue. Then write the word made by the boxed letters. It tells you something you might say at dinner time.

role	nutrients	energy	decay
cycle	relationship	consume	

1. something that happens again and again ___ ___ ___ ☐ ___

2. an important job ___ ___ ___ ☐

3. these make you strong ___ ___ ☐ ___ ___ ___ ___ ___

4. to take something in ___ ___ ___ ☐ ___ ___ ___

5. the power to do things ☐ ___ ___ ___ ___ ___

6. to rot ___ ___ ___ ☐ ___

7. a connection ___ ___ ___ ☐ ___ ___ ___ ___ ___ ___

Answer: ___ ___ ___ ´ ___   ___ ___ ___ !

Word Challenge: Which Word?

With a partner, take turns saying the words listed below. Together, think of a statement for each one that gives a strong clue about its meaning. Write your statement next to the word. The first one has been done for you.

1 cause _"I make things happen."_

2 example _____

3 energy _____

4 produce _____

Word Challenge: What's Your Answer?

Take turns with a partner reading each question out loud and writing an answer on the line. Answer the questions in complete sentences. The first one has been done for you.

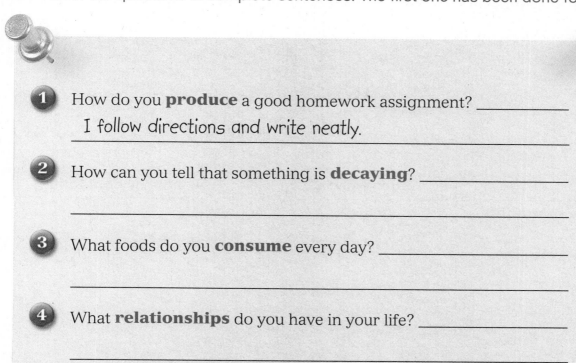

1 How do you **produce** a good homework assignment? _____
I follow directions and write neatly.

2 How can you tell that something is **decaying**? _____
_____

3 What foods do you **consume** every day? _____
_____

4 What **relationships** do you have in your life? _____
_____

Word Connections

In the spaces at the top of the wheel, write the words from the box that connect to the center word or idea. In the shaded spaces at the bottom of the wheel, write the words that do not connect. Discuss your answers with a partner.

cycle	decay	energy	nutrients	cause	example

YES

consume

NO

Word Study: The Suffixes *-able* and *-ible*

When the suffix *-able* or *-ible* is added to a verb such as *consume*, it does two things:
- First, it makes the verb an adjective: *consumable*.
- Second, it changes the word's meaning. The word now describes something that can be eaten or used up.

Drop the *-e* from the end of a word before adding *-able* or *-ible*.

A. Write each word's root verb and suffix. Use a dictionary if you need help.

	Root Word	+ *-able* or *-ible* Suffix?
1 consumable		
2 producible		

B. Complete each sentence with a word from the chart.

1 Bananas are_____ only in warm places.

2 Something we can eat or drink is _____ .

30

The Language of Testing

How would you answer a question like this on a test?

What is the **purpose of** nutrients?

    A. They provide moisture to plants.
    B. They help plants and animals grow.
    C. They help break down dead plants.
    D. They provide oxygen for the blood.

💡 **Tip**

The word *purpose* can mean *reason* or *use*.

Test Strategy: If you see a question that uses the word purpose, rewrite it using the words reason or use.

1 How could you say the question above in a different way?

_____

_____

Try the strategy again by asking these questions in a different way.

2 What is the purpose of decomposition?

    A. It breaks down dead matter.
    B. It allows animals to feed off the dead plants.
    C. Reproduction takes place there.
    D. It creates a way for animals to adapt to changing climates.

3 What is the main purpose of photosynthesis?

    A. to create oxygen
    B. to use carbon dioxide
    C. to produce energy for plants
    D. to produce energy for animals

_____   _____

_____   _____

_____   _____

In Your Vocabulary Journal

Find each of these words in your Science Vocabulary Journal. Working by yourself or with a partner, use the definitions from pages 26 and 27 of your Work Text to complete the rest of the entry for each word.

cause	**consume**	**cycle**	**decay**	**energy**
example	**nutrients**	**produce**	**relationship**	**role**

Lesson 6 Ecosystems

Read the passage below. Think about the meaning of the words printed in **bold**. Underline any words that start with *eco-* or end with *-ity*. Write what you think each word means near it. Remember that *eco-* names a place in nature, and *-ity* names a way of being. The first one has been done for you.

Your Own Special World

Vocabulary Strategy

Use prefixes and suffixes you know to help you understand the meanings of new words.

system in nature

You can create your own world in a terrarium. A terrarium is actually a **habitat** in which small plants and animals can live together. It is like an **ecosystem** in a bottle!

To make a terrarium, you'll need a large glass or plastic bottle. Fill the bottom with a layer of small rocks or pebbles. Add potting soil for the next layer.

Next, choose the kind of **environment** you want. You could have a dry environment, like a desert. Or, you could have warm and wet, or **tropical** environment. Choose plants that grow well together in your environment. Place each plant in damp soil. Then put your terrarium in an area that gets a lot of light, but not too much.

Once you have the plants, you might want to add a toad or snail. Now you have your own **community** in a bottle.

New Science Words

community
noun   a group of plants, animals, or people living in the same area

ecosystem
noun   the plants, animals, and nonliving things in an area that have a relationship with one another

environment
noun   the natural world of land, sea, and air and the things that affect it

habitat
noun   the natural place where a plant or animal lives and grows

tropical
adjective   having to do with the tropics, a very hot and wet area of the earth

Now read this passage and look for prefixes or suffixes to help you understand the words in **bold**. Circle any words that end with -*al*, -*ation*, and -*ist*. Write what you think each circled word means next to it. Remember that –*al* names a connection, -*ation* names a process, and –*ist* names someone who does a certain thing.

The Gobi Desert

Most people think a **desert** is a very hot place. In fact, one of the earth's largest deserts is also its coldest. The summer temperature there is usually around 70°F. The winter temperature is usually an icy 10°F. That's hardly tropical weather! Welcome to China's Gobi desert.

The Gobi desert covers over a half-million square miles. The soil is dry and mostly rocky. Much of the Gobi gets less than ten inches of rain or snow a year. There are not many trees, so there are no **forests**. Instead, many different kinds of grasses grow in the Gobi desert.

Do you think you'd like to live in the Gobi desert? The **population** is small. Most people live around the edges of the desert where more rain falls. Other people move from place to place looking for water and food for their sheep and cattle. Scientists believe people have lived in the Gobi for thousands of years.

Tired of ice and snow, Pedro found the Gobi **desert** a nice change.

More New Science Words

desert

  noun   a dry area of land with few plants

forest

  noun   a large area of land where many trees grow close together

population

  noun   the number of plants, animals, or humans that live in a certain area

Other Useful Words

examine

  verb   to look at or check something very carefully

method

  noun   a certain way of doing something

Use the Strategy

Look at a chapter in your science textbook that your teacher identifies. Use prefixes and suffixes you know to help you figure out the meanings of any new words you find.

The Right Word

Read each sentence. Look at the word or phrase that is underlined. Write one of the words from the box that means the same or almost the same as the underlined part of the sentence. Discuss your answers with a partner.

desert	population	tropical	examined

1 _____ The <u>number of people living in the area</u> had grown in the past two years.

2 _____ The doctor <u>studied</u> his patient carefully.

3 _____ We almost ran out of water as we traveled across the <u>hot, dry area</u>.

4 _____ After the cool weather, the <u>warm, wet</u> weather felt great.

environment	forest	habitat	method

5 _____ The tiger was pushed out of its <u>natural home</u> by new villages.

6 _____ Petra had a <u>certain way</u> for making a sandwich.

7 _____ During the hike, we walked through a <u>thick area of trees</u>.

8 _____ Everyone should work to keep the <u>air, land, and water we live in</u> clean.

Word Challenge: True or False

Take turns with a partner reading the sentences below out loud. Write **T** next to each sentence that is true. Write **F** next to each sentence that is false. Rewrite each false sentence. The first one has been done for you.

1. _F_ A **tropical** climate is usually very cool and dry.

   A tropical climate is usually very warm and wet.

2. _____ Some scientists follow the **population** of dolphins.

   _____

3. _____ A **forest** has no trees and many wildflowers.

   _____

4. _____ The **habitat** of most fish is in a desert.

   _____

Word Challenge: What's Your Answer?

Take turns with a partner reading each question out loud and writing an answer on the line. Answer the questions with complete sentences. The first one has been done for you.

1. How would you feel if you were in a **desert**? Why? _I would be_
   hot and thirsty, because a desert is hot and dry.

2. What is your favorite **environment**? Why? _____

   _____

3. What is the **population** of your classroom? How do you know?

   _____

4. Who is an important member of your community? Why is he or she important?

   _____

35

Analogies

Use a word from the box to finish each sentence. Write the word on the line. Discuss your answers with a partner.

desert	forest	examine	tropical

1. Ocean is to wet as _____ is to dry.

2. Book is to library as tree is to _____.

3. Heat is to _____ as cold is to arctic.

4. Eye is to _____ as ear is to listen.

Word Study: The Prefix *inter-*

When the prefix *inter-* is added to a noun such as *forest,* it changes the noun's meaning.
- First, it makes the noun an adjective: *interforest.*
- Second, it adds *between* or *among* to the word's meaning.

forest (n.) a large area of land where many trees grow close together
interforest (adj.) between or among forests

A. Circle the *inter-* words in the story.

     Joanie and Kim were ready to go. They were leaving to do intercommunity science studies. An airplane would take them on an interecosystem trip. First, they would learn about the interforest flight of birds. Then they would study the interdesert travels of people. Then they would write a paper about what they learned.

B. Fill each blank with an *inter-* word from the story.

1. The word _____ means "between deserts."

2. When birds fly between forests, their flight is _____.

3. Their _____ studies took Joanie and Kim to many places.

36

The Language of Testing

How would you answer a question like this on a test?

A large area in North Africa rarely receives any rainfall. What does this statement **suggest**?

    A. It is probably a good place for farming.
    B. It is probably a desert climate.
    C. It is probably near mountains.
    D. It is probably a tropical climate.

 Tip

When *suggest* is used in a question, you should draw a conclusion about the information in the question.

Test Strategy: If you see a question that uses the word *suggest*, rewrite it so that it asks you what the information in the question probably means.

1 How could you say the question above in a different way?

_____

_____

Try the strategy again by asking these questions in a different way.

2 What does it suggest about an area if the population is growing quickly?

    A. The area is a big city.
    B. The weather is good.
    C. People are attracted to something in the area.
    D. The area had few people.

3 Many plants in an area were slowly dying. What does this suggest?

    A. The ecosystem is in trouble.
    B. The plants need a new habitat.
    C. There isn't much soil.
    D. There are too many animals.

_____   _____

_____   _____

_____   _____

In Your Vocabulary Journal

Find each of these words in your Science Vocabulary Journal. Working by yourself or with a partner, use the definitions from pages 32 and 33 of your Work Text to complete the rest of the entry for each word.

community	desert	ecosystem	environment	examine
forest	habitat	method	population	tropical

Lesson 7 Inside the Earth

Read the passage below. Think about the meanings of the new words printed in **bold**. Underline any examples or descriptions you find that might help you figure out what these words mean. The first one has been done for you.

Science Fact or Science Fiction?

Vocabulary Strategy

Look for examples and descriptions in a text to help you figure out the meanings of new words. Look for clues, like *example*, *like*, or *such as*. Look for pictures that show what a new word means, too.

Jules Verne was a writer who lived in the 1800s. His stories were filled with adventures that were based on science. Many of his books are still popular today. One of his books is *A Journey to the Center of the Earth*.

This book is about a scientist who travels under the earth's **crust**. <u>This crust is very much like the top crust on a pie.</u> The scientist believes he can reach the earth's **core**, which is like the core at the center of an apple. Instead, he finds an underground ocean. Today, scientists know that between the crust and core is a layer called the **mantle**. This mantle is made up of very hot rock, not water.

In the book, the scientist also meets dinosaurs. In the real world he would find only **fossils**, like the ones we see today in museums. Much of Jules Verne's science was more fiction than fact. However, he could still tell a great story.

New Science Words

core
noun   the very center part of the earth

crust
noun   the outer layer of the earth

fossil
noun   the parts of dead plants or animals that have turned into rock

mantle
noun   the layer of the earth between the center and the outer crust

Now read this passage and practice the vocabulary strategy again. Underline examples and descriptions in the passage. Draw an arrow from each one to the new word it describes.

It's Elemental

Scientists have discovered 110 elements in the world. An element is made up completely of one thing. If you take it apart to its smallest, tiniest piece, every part of the element will be the same. Everything in the world is made up of those 110 elements.

Some elements like gold are worth a lot of money. Other elements like **oxygen** and **nitrogen** are as free as the air. In fact, they're part of the air you breathe.

Other elements are called **minerals**. These elements are hard and solid. Some minerals are dark like rock. Others are crystals that you can see through, almost like glass.

Carbon is a mineral that is sometimes like a rock and sometimes like a crystal. Coal and diamond are both examples of carbon. We sometimes cook with coal and use it to heat our homes. We use diamonds to make jewelry.

More New Science Words

carbon
  noun a material found in the earth that is necessary for life

mineral
  noun a nonliving material found in nature such as salt, iron, and silver

nitrogen
  noun a colorless material found in nature in the air and in the soil

oxygen
  noun a colorless material in the air that is needed by most life

Other Useful Words

conduct
  verb to plan and do something

record
  verb to put information in writing
  noun information that has been saved

"Well, a diamond is really just **carbon**!"

Use the Strategy

Look at a chapter in your science textbook that your teacher identifies. Use examples, descriptions, and pictures to help you figure out the meaning of any new words you find.

39

Finish the Sentence

Use a word from the box to finish each sentence. Write the correct word on the line. Discuss your choices with a partner.

| core | fossil | mineral | oxygen |

1 We found a _____ of an insect in the stone.

2 She hollowed out the center of the fruit down to its _____.

3 Animals need _____ to breathe.

4 Iron is a _____ that is found in nature.

| crust | recorded | carbon | mantle |

5 Eli's grandfather _____ their family history in a notebook.

6 The frozen lake had a _____ of ice on the top.

7 The wood burned down to a block of _____ that looked like coal.

8 Hot rock is in the _____ of the earth.

Word Challenge: Which Word?

With a partner, take turns saying the words listed below. Together, think of a statement for each one that gives a clue about its meaning. Write your statement next to the word. The first one has been done for you.

1 **core** _"I am the center of the earth!"_

2 **carbon** _____

3 **fossil** _____

4 **nitrogen** _____

Word Challenge: Correct or Incorrect

Take turns reading the sentences below out loud. Write **C** if the sentence is correct, and write **I** if the sentence is incorrect. Rewrite the incorrect sentences. The first one has been done for you.

1 __I__ We made a drawing showing the earth's outer layer, the **core**.

We made a drawing showing the earth's center, the core.

2 _____ Some of Earth's **minerals** are rubber, sugar, and wood.

_____

3 _____ He was having trouble breathing, so they gave him **oxygen**.

_____

4 _____ A notebook is a good place to **record** important information.

_____

41

Word Pairs

Choose the pair of words from each group that best completes each sentence. Write the words on the lines. Discuss your choices with a partner.

1 Both _____ and _____ are found in the air.

      carbon   **oxygen**   **mineral**   **nitrogen**

2 _____ is one type of _____.

      mineral   **mantle**   **oxygen**   **carbon**

3 Both the _____ and the _____ are below the surface of the earth.

      mantle   **crust**   **record**   **core**

4 You can use a notebook to _____ the results when you _____ an experiment.

      mineral   **conduct**   **fossil**   **record**

Word Study: The Suffix -ation

When the suffix -ation is added to a noun such as oxygen, it changes the noun's meaning. The new word means "the process of adding oxygen to something."

oxygen (n.) a colorless mineral in the air that is needed by most life
oxygenation (n.) the process or result of adding oxygen

A. Add the suffix -ation to each element name to make a new word. Use a dictionary to check your spelling and definitions.

	Element	+ -ation	Meaning
1	oxygen		
2	nitrogen		
3	carbon		

B. Write a new -ation word in each blank.

1 The process of adding carbon dioxide to soda pop is called _____.

2 Fish breathe oxygen that plants add to water by _____.

The Language of Testing

How would you answer a question like this on a test?

What is something that (compares closely to) nitrogen?

    A. water
    B. air
    C. oxygen
    D. carbon

 Tip

Compares closely to means *is most like*.

Test Strategy: If you see a question with the phrase *compares closely to* on a test, rewrite it using the phrase *is most like*.

1 How would you say the above question a different way?

_____

_____

Try the strategy again by asking these questions in a different way.

2 What compares closely to *crust*?

    A. inner layer
    B. center layer
    C. outer layer
    D. topsoil

3 Which animal compares most closely to a frog?

    A. toad
    B. lizard
    C. salamander
    D. newt

_____

_____

_____

_____

_____

_____

In Your Vocabulary Journal

Find each of these words in your Science Vocabulary Journal. Working by yourself or with a partner, use the definitions from pages 38 and 39 of your Work Text to complete the rest of the entry for each word.

carbon	conduct	core	crust	fossil
mantle	mineral	nitrogen	oxygen	record

Lesson 8

The Changing Earth

Read the passage below. Think about the meanings of the new words printed in **bold**. Circle each definition, and draw a line to the word it describes. The first one has been done for you.

Mount St. Helens

Vocabulary Strategy

Look for definitions in the text to help you understand the meanings of new words.

Mount St. Helens is in the state of Washington. It isn't just any mountain, however. It is a **volcano**. (Volcanoes are mountains that erupt, or explode.) In 1980, Mount St. Helens erupted. The explosion actually blew the top off the mountain. It left a large hole called a crater. A large area around the volcano was covered with ash.

Hot **lava**, or melted rock, ash, and gasses deep in the earth escape through volcanoes. Sometimes volcanoes erupt because of an **earthquake**. During an earthquake, the outer layer of the earth shifts or moves.

This movement makes the ground shake. It also allows melted rock to come out of the ground.

There are many volcanoes on the North American **continent**. Mount St. Helens was the first volcano to erupt in the main part of the United States since 1917.

New Science Words

continent
noun   one of seven large areas of land on Earth

earthquake
noun   when the ground shakes because the outer layer of the earth is moving

lava
noun   hot, melted rock found deep in the earth

volcano
noun   a mountain that sometimes erupts, letting melted rock, ash, and gas come out of the earth

Now read this passage and practice the vocabulary strategy again. Underline any definitions in the passage that help you figure out what the new words in **bold** mean.

The Ice Age

About 12,000 years ago, much of the earth was covered with ice. Giant **glaciers** covered the northern part of the United States. A glacier is a huge, slowly moving sheet of ice. As the glaciers moved, they caused **erosion**. When ice, water, or wind wear away soil or rock, it is called erosion. The erosion shaped the earth's **surface**, or outer layer.

When the glaciers melted, they left behind dirt and rock. This **sediment** was very rich in minerals. That's why the soil in some parts of the country is so good for farming. The glaciers dug out valleys as they moved. Water from the melted glaciers filled the valleys. These became rivers and lakes.

Scientists think that the seas were 300 feet lower during the Ice Age. That's as deep as a football field is long! This is because so much water was frozen in the glaciers. Ice Age glaciers were thousands of miles wide and over a mile thick. That's a lot of ice!

More New Science Words

erosion
  noun   the wearing away of dirt or rock by wind, ice, or water

glacier
  noun   a huge, slowly moving sheet of ice

sediment
  noun   sand and dirt at the bottom of a river or lake, or that is left behind by moving water

surface
  noun   the top or outside layer of something

Other Useful Words

effect
  noun   a change that results from some action

recognize
  verb   to know what something is because of its features

Use the Strategy

Look at a chapter in your textbook that your teacher identifies. Use definitions in the text to help you figure out the meaning of any new words you find.

Matching

Finish the sentences in Group A with words from Group B. Write the letter of the word on the line. Discuss your choices with a partner.

Group A

1 Deep grooves formed on the hillside where moving water had caused _____.

2 The top layer or _____ of the earth has valleys, mountains, and hills.

3 The movement caused by the _____ hurt several buildings.

4 One icy _____ in Alaska is almost 50 miles wide.

Group B

A. earthquake
B. erosion
C. glacier
D. surface

Group A

5 Hot _____ flowed down the side of the mountain.

6 The delicious smell of baking pies had the _____ of making me hungry.

7 The _____ in the river came from soil that was washed in by the rain.

8 I didn't _____ him because he was wearing a mask.

Group B

E. effect
F. recognize
G. sediment
H. lava

Word Challenge: Finish the Idea

With a partner, take turns reading the incomplete sentences below. Write an ending for each. The first one has been done for you.

1. We knew we were in an **earthquake** because _the ground was moving up_ _and down._

2. The United States is not a **continent** because _____ _____

3. We knew that the mountain was a **volcano** because _____ _____

4. Mom didn't **recognize** me because _____ _____

Word Challenge: What's Your Answer?

Take turns with a partner reading each question out loud and writing an answer on the line. Answer the questions in complete sentences. The first one has been done for you.

1. What in your town is an example of **erosion**? _The deep grooves in_ _the side of the hill are an example of erosion._

2. What might be the **effect** of eating twenty candy bars? _____ _____

3. Where would you find **sediment**? _____ _____

4. Describe the **surface** of your desk. _____ _____

Word Pairs

Choose the pair of words from each group that best completes each sentence. Write the words on the lines. Discuss your choices with a partner.

1 There was _____ in the water from all the _____.

        continent   **erosion**   **effects**   **sediment**

2 Part of the _____ was covered by a _____ during the Ice Age.

        continent   **earthquake**   **glacier**   **volcano**

3 During the _____, the _____ of the earth moved.

        earthquake   **lava**   **volcano**   **surface**

4 Scientists could tell the mountain was a _____ even though there was no _____.

        erosion   **earthquake**   **lava**   **volcano**

Word Study: The Suffix -ology and -ologist

When suffixes -ology and -ologist are added to nouns such as *glacier*, they change the noun's meaning.

- -ology means "the study of": *glaciology*
- -ologist adds the means "a person who studies": *glaciologist*

> **glacier** (n.) a huge, slowly moving sheet of ice
> **glaciology** (n.) the study of glaciers
> **glaciologist** (n.) a person who studies glaciers

A. Add -ology and -ologist to the words below. You may use a dictionary to check your spelling.

	+ -ology	+ -ologist
1 sediment		
2 volcano		
3 mineral		

B. Write a sentence for one of the -ology words and one of the -ologist words you made. Make sure your sentences show that you understand what each word means.

1 _____

2 _____

The Language of Testing

How would you answer a question like this on a test?

What was a **major effect** of the flooding?

    A. New levees were built.
    B. Most of the crops were lost.
    C. Erosion made the bridge collapse.
    D. All of the above.

 Tip

Major effect means something very important happened because of or as a result of something else.

Test Strategy: If you see a question that uses the phrase *major effect*, notice what comes after it. It is usually an important event. What happened because of this thing or event? Read each answer, and add to it *because of the* (event). You can use this to test which answers are right or wrong.

1 What phrase would you use to test each answer choice above?

_____

_____

Try the strategy again by adding a test phrase to the answer choices below. Write your test phrase below each question.

2 What was a major effect of the Ice Age?

    A. The sea level rose.
    B. Melting ice caused earthquakes.
    C. Glaciers changed Earth's surface.
    D. People migrated from Asia.

_____

_____

_____

3 What is a major effect of water freezing and melting?

    A. Rock cracks or breaks apart.
    B. Beaches are washed away.
    C. Erosion removes the topsoil.
    D. Waterways become clogged.

_____

_____

_____

In Your Vocabulary Journal

Find each of these words in your Science Vocabulary Journal. Working by yourself or with a partner, use the definitions from pages 44 and 45 of your Work Text to complete the rest of the entry for each word.

continent	**earthquake**	**effect**	**erosion**	**glacier**
lava	**recognize**	**sediment**	**surface**	**volcano**

Read the passage below. Think about the meanings of the new words printed in **bold**. Create connections between the new words and words you know. These will help you remember what the new words mean. Write these connections near the new words in the passage. The first one has been done for you.

Calendars

the sun

Vocabulary Strategy

Create connections between new words and words you know. You can use a Word Anchor chart to help you create connections.

In the past, calendars were based on the sun and the moon. **Solar** calendars followed the sun's path in the sky. People noticed that sometimes the sun was higher in the sky. Sometimes it was lower. From this, they figured out the number of days in a year. Today we know that the earth spins around an imaginary line or **axis**. The axis is tilted. So the sun appears in different places in the sky during different seasons.

Lunar calendars were based on the **phases** of the moon. For example, a full moon and new moon are two of the phases.

In these calendars, a month was about 29 days long.

In the calendar we use today, each year has 12 months and 365 days. But don't forget leap year, which has 366 days!

New Science Words

axis
noun   an imaginary line that runs through the center of something

lunar
adjective   having to do with the moon

phase
noun   a stage in the way the moon looks from Earth

solar
adjective   having to do with the sun

Now read this passage and practice the vocabulary strategies again. Write near the new words any connections you can use to "anchor" the meaning of the new words.

Galileo

Galileo was an Italian scientist. He lived in the late 1500s and early 1600s. He built the first telescope, a tool that a scientist can use to look closely at the sky. Using his telescope, Galileo figured out that the earth moves in an **orbit** around the sun. An orbit is like a curved path or circle.

Galileo also discovered that the earth **revolves**, or spins around. He also saw that **planets**, like Earth, had **satellites**. An example of a satellite is a moon that orbits around a planet. He saw four of the moons that orbit the planet Jupiter through his telescope.

Today, people who study the planets and stars use a telescope like Galileo's. They also have tools that help them **measure** things in space. Without Galileo's ideas, scientists today would find it pretty hard to **explore**, or learn about the sky.

More New Science Words

orbit

noun   the curved path an object makes around a larger object

verb   to travel in a curved path around something

planet

noun   a large rock, such as Earth, that moves around a star

revolve

verb   to spin in a circle around a center

satellite

noun   an object that moves around a larger object in space

"Are you sure this is the best way to **measure** a **planet**?"

Other Useful Words

explore

verb   to learn about something, or to travel through an unknown area to learn about it

measure

verb   to figure out the size of an object or how far two places are from each other

Use the Strategy

Look at a chapter in your textbook that your teacher identifies. Use associations to help you anchor the meanings of any new words you find.

Finish the Paragraph

Use the words in **bold** to finish the paragraph below. Write the correct word in the blank. One word will not be used. Discuss your choices with a partner.

exploring   **axis**   **lunar**   **orbits**   **planets**

revolve   **satellite**   **Solar**   **measure**   **phases**

Our class is _____ **(1)** space. Since we could not travel there, we

built a model. We have nine _____ **(2)** and each one moves around, or

_____ **(3)**, the sun. We have a moon, or _____ **(4)**,

that orbits Earth. Our model of Earth can actually spin on its _____ **(5)**!

Last week, we took the model to another class. We told them that our model

was called the _____ **(6)** System. It is called this because all of

the planets orbit the sun. The teacher told us that the root word for *solar* is *sol*,

which means *sun*. She also said that *luna* means *moon*. So *luna* is the root word

for _____ **(7)**. The moon goes through many stages, or

_____ **(8)** each month. Next week, we want to learn how scientists

_____ **(9)** the distance between stars. I hope I have a big enough ruler!

52

Word Challenge: Finish the Idea

With a partner, take turns reading the incomplete sentences below. Write an ending for each. The first one has been done for you.

1 Mars is my favorite **planet** because ___it is red and very hot.___

2 I would love to **explore** Jupiter because _____

_____

3 I would not like living on a **satellite** because _____

_____

4 Some people use **solar** energy because _____

_____

Word Challenge: True or False

Take turns with a partner reading the sentences below out loud. Write **T** next to each sentence that is true. Write **F** next to each sentence that is false. Rewrite the false sentences. The first one has been done for you.

1 __T__ The earth **revolves** once every 24 hours.

2 _____ A normal **orbit** is a straight line.

_____

3 _____ During each **phase**, the moon looks the same.

_____

4 _____ If something is **lunar**, it has to do with the moon.

_____

Word Connections

In the spaces at the top of the wheel, write the words from the box that connect to the center word or idea. In the shaded spaces at the bottom of the wheel, write the words that do not connect. Discuss your answers with a partner.

| axis | lunar | orbit | planet | satellite | solar |

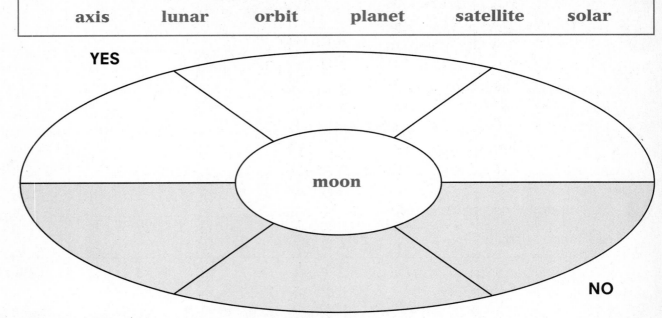

YES

moon

NO

Word Study: The Prefix *non-*

When the prefix *non-* is added to an adjective such as *lunar,* it changes the adjective's meaning. The new word now means the opposite of the old word. *Non-* can mean *not* or *without*.

lunar (adj.) having to do with the moon
nonlunar (adj.) having nothing to do with the moon

A. Add the prefix *non-* to each word to make a new word. Write your own definition for each. Use a dictionary to check your spelling and your definitions.

	+ *non-*	Meaning
1 solar		
2 example		
3 sense		

B. Write your own sentences using two words from the chart.

1 _____

2 _____

54

The Language of Testing

How would you answer a question like this on a test?

The Planets

Name	Diameter	Distance from Sun
Mercury	3,032 miles	36 million miles
Venus	7,519 miles	67 million miles
Earth	7,926 miles	93 million miles

Source: factmonster.com

 Based on the table, which planet is the smallest?

A. Earth
B. Jupiter
C. Mercury
D. Pluto

Tip

When you see the words *based on* in a question, it means you need to look at a map, chart, or picture to answer the question.

Test Strategy: Circle or underline words or phrases in the question that tell you what to do. In the question above you would circle or underline *based on the table*. You can also rewrite the question to tell you to *look at the table to find the information you need.*

1 How could you say the question above in a different way?

_____

_____

Try the strategy again by asking these questions in a different way.

2 Based on the table, which planet has the most moons?

A. Earth
B. Jupiter
C. Saturn
D. Neptune

_____

_____

_____

3 Based on the diagram, what are the two kinds of comet tails?

A. dust and oxygen
B. ion and carbon
C. dust and ion
D. nitrogen and atomic

_____

_____

_____

In Your Vocabulary Journal

Find each of these words in your Science Vocabulary Journal. Working by yourself or with a partner, use the definitions from pages 50 and 51 of your Work Text to complete the rest of the entry for each word.

axis	**explore**	**lunar**	**measure**	**orbit**
phase	**planet**	**revolve**	**satellite**	**solar**

Lesson 10 Weather

Read the passage below. Think about the meanings of the new words printed in **bold**. Circle any synonyms, or words that might mean the same as the new words. Draw an arrow from each synonym to the new word it describes. The first one has been done for you.

TV Weather

Vocabulary Strategy

Use synonyms, or words that mean about the same as the new words to help you understand their meaning. Look for clues like *or* to help you find synonyms in a text.

When you watch the weather on TV, you often see a weather person pointing to a map. This map is covered with symbols. For example, a **front**, or edge of a mass of cold or warm air, is shown by a line and arrows. A large *L* on the map means that there is a low **pressure** system nearby. In a low pressure system, the air isn't pressing down strongly. Sometimes, a drawing of a large **thermometer** pops up. The large thermometer tells the **temperature**, or how hot or cold it is outside.

During the show, the weather person sees only a green wall. A computer adds the maps, symbols, and **labels** later. So how do weather people know what to point to? They watch another television that you can't see! Next time you watch the weather on TV, try to catch the weather person watching TV, too!

New Science Words

front
noun   the edge of a mass of warm or cold air

pressure
noun   the effect of one thing pushing on another

temperature
noun   the amount of warmth in something

thermometer
noun   a tool for measuring how warm something is

Now read this passage and practice the vocabulary strategy again. Circle any synonyms and draw an arrow from each to the word it describes.

Water, Water, Everywhere

Water is always changing. One major change is when water turns into air. This is called **evaporation**. Water in rivers, lakes, oceans, and even in the ground evaporates into the **atmosphere**. The atmosphere is the mass of air around the earth. In the atmosphere, wetness or **humidity** makes clouds. When the clouds touch cooler air, the water becomes rain or snow. The water falls back to Earth and the changes begin again.

There are some places that have a dry **climate**. In a dry climate, water in the air doesn't come back down as rain or snow. The water in these areas still evaporates, however. Can you **predict** or guess where it goes? It goes up into the atmosphere and falls down again as rain or snow somewhere else. It's all part of the cycle.

"Drink the water quickly, before it **evaporates**!"

More New Science Words

atmosphere
  noun   the layer of air around the earth

climate
  noun   the usual weather of a large area

evaporation
  noun   the way in which water seems to disappear into the air

humidity
  noun   the amount of wetness in the air

Other Useful Words

label
  verb   to place a name on something

predict
  verb   to say what will happen

Use the Strategy

Look at a chapter in your textbook that your teacher identifies. Use synonyms in the text to help you figure out the meaning of any new words you find. Keep track of the new words and synonyms in a chart.

The Right Word

Read each sentence. Look at the word or phrase that is underlined. Write one of the words from the box that means the same or almost the same thing as the underlined part of the sentence. Discuss your answers with a partner.

thermometer	humidity	front	pressure

1 _____   The <u>wetness in the air</u> made it feel warmer than it was.

2 _____   The <u>tool that shows how warm it is</u> read 98.6°.

3 _____   The <u>edge of a mass of cold air</u> moved down from Canada.

4 _____   I couldn't keep the door closed because the <u>pushing</u> of the wind was too strong.

temperature	label	predict	climate

5 _____   The <u>usual weather</u> in a desert is hot and dry.

6 _____   We had to <u>name</u> the parts of the frog.

7 _____   The <u>amount of hot or cold</u> dropped to freezing last night.

8 _____   How are scientists able to <u>guess</u> when big storms are going to happen?

Word Challenge: Would You Rather . . .

Take turns with a partner reading the questions below out loud. Think of a response and write it on the line. Write your responses in complete sentences. The first one has been done for you.

1. Would you rather feel high **humidity** or low humidity? Why? _I'd rather feel high_ _humidity because places with low humidity are too dry._

2. Would you rather **predict** the weather or the future? Why? _____

   _____

3. Would you rather live in a freezing cold or a boiling hot **climate**? Why? _____

   _____

4. Would you rather have a warm **front** or a cold front move through your area? Why?

   _____

   _____

Word Challenge: Word Relationships

Take turns with a partner reading the groups of words below. Write the word from the lesson that best goes with each group. The first one has been done for you.

1. ____thermometer____ measure, numbers, temperature

2. _____ weight, push

3. _____ water, dry, disappear

4. _____ warmth, fever, thermometer

Extend the Meaning

Write the letter of the word or phrase that best completes each sentence. Discuss your choices with a partner.

1 Another word for **atmosphere** would be _____.
  a lunar
  b. ecosystem
  c. air

2 If it was hot and **humid** you might _____.
  a. feel sleepy
  b. feel sweaty
  c. increase your exercise

3 When a **front** passes through, _____.
  a. the weather stays the same
  b. it usually starts to rain
  c. the weather usually changes

4 You would feel **pressure** if _____.
  a. someone squeezed your arm
  b. you got a flat tire on your bike
  c. it started to rain very hard

Word Study: The -ed Ending

The -ed ending is added to a root verb when talking about what happened in the past. If the verb ends in
- -e, just add -d: evaporated.
- a short vowel and a consonant, double the consonant. Then add -ed: labelled.

> **evaporate** (v.) to make water go into the air
> **evaporated** (v., past tense) to have made water go into the air

A. Add **-ed** to the words below. Write a definition for each new word. You may use a dictionary to check your spelling and definitions.

		+ **-ed**	**Meaning**
1	label		
2	predict		
3	pressure		

B. Fill the blanks with -ed words from the chart.

Carlos reads weather reports for a TV news show. Here is the report that he read

on Thursday night: "I was right when I _____ rain for Wednesday

night. It rained all night! I predict more rain for Friday. It will fall north of our city. I

have _____ those areas on the map. Good night, everyone."

The Language of Testing

How would you answer a question like this on a test?

Which of the following terms is
associated with weather?

    A. evaporation
    B. thermometer
    C. earthquake
    D. carbon

 Tip

When *associated with* is used in question, it means the same thing as *related to* or *connected to*.

Test Strategy: If you see a question that contains the phrase *associated with*, rewrite it using the phrases *related to* or *connected to*.

1 How could you say the question above in a different way?

_____

_____

Try the strategy again by asking these questions in a different way.

2 Which is associated with the atmosphere?

    A. air
    B. temperature
    C. sunlight
    D. phases of the moon

3 What is associated with the movement of weather patterns?

    A. humidity
    B. evaporation
    C. the water cycle
    D. front

_____

_____

_____

_____

_____

_____

In Your Vocabulary Journal

Find each of these words in your Science Vocabulary Journal. Working by yourself or with a partner, use the definitions from pages 56 and 57 of your Work Text to complete the rest of the entry for each word.

atmosphere	climate	evaporation	front	humidity
label	predict	pressure	temperature	thermometer

Read the passage below. Think about the meaning of the words printed in **bold**. Circle any words that begin with *en-* or *ex-*. Write what you think each word means near it. Remember that the prefix *en-* means *in*, and *ex-* means *out*. The first one has been done for you.

Copper Country

Vocabulary Strategy

Use prefixes and suffixes you know to help you understand the meanings of new words.

A certain part of Michigan is called copper country. That is because there are so many **deposits**, or natural layers, of copper there. Long ago, Native Americans discovered the copper. Much of it was on the earth's surface.

Around 1840, people began to dig deep mines to *take out* → **extract** the copper from the ground. Thousands of people came to Michigan hoping to make a lot of money with the copper.

The mines caused a lot of **pollution** that dirtied the soil and the water. The owners of the mines also did nothing to **enrich**

the land after taking so much out of it. As the copper ran out, most people moved away. Today, old mine shafts and ghost towns dot the landscape in what was once copper country.

New Science Words

deposit

noun natural layers of something that build up over time

enrich

verb to make something better by adding other things

extract

verb to take something out of something else

pollution

noun something that dirties and harms the water, soil, and air

Now read this passage and underline any words that begin with *re-* or end in *-able*. Write what you think each underlined word means next to it. Remember that *re-* means "to do again," and that *–able* tells you what something can do or have done to it.

The Three R's of the Environment

Have you ever heard of the three *R*'s of the environment? They are **reduce**, reuse, and **recycle**. Many people believe that you can help reduce pollution if you follow the three *R*'s. But just what do they mean?

The first *R*, *reduce*, means that you should use less of everything. You should buy things with less packaging. You should use less water. You should also use less gas and electricity.

The second *R*, *reuse*, means that you shouldn't just use something once and throw it away. Having **reusable** things means you use a lunch box over and over again. It means you take your grocery bags back to the market. It means washing a plastic spoon instead of throwing it out.

The third *R*, *recycle*, means that you don't put anything in the trash that can be recycled. You can recycle glass, paper, and many plastic items. This way we **conserve** our natural resources.

Jacob couldn't see that he was part of the problem.

More New Science Words

conserve
 verb   to use something carefully so it will last longer
recycle
 verb   to use something over again, sometimes in a different way
reduce
 verb   to make the amount of something less or smaller
reusable
 adjective   can be used more than one time

Other Useful Words

communicate
 verb   to share information through speaking, writing, or movements
purpose
 noun   the reason for doing something

Use the Strategy

Look at a chapter in your textbook that your teacher identifies. Use prefixes and suffixes you know to help you figure out the meaning of any new words you find.

Extend the Meaning

Write the letter of the word or phrase that best completes each sentence. Discuss your answers with a partner.

1 When we _____ something, we're careful how much we use.

    a. conserve

    b. extract

    c. reduce

2 We tried to _____ the amount of gasoline we use.

    a. enrich

    b. reduce

    c. recycle

3 Dogs _____ by barking and wagging their tails.

    a. recycle

    b. conserve

    c. communicate

4 Miners _____ minerals such as copper, coal, and gold from the earth.

    a. enrich

    b. extract

    c. recycle

5 The _____, or reason, for turning off the lights is to save energy.

    a. pollution

    b. purpose

    c. deposit

6 The _____ was so bad that the air looked brown.

    a. pollution

    b. deposits

    c. reduce

7 In 1849, large _____ of gold were found in California.

    a. pollution

    b. deposits

    c. extract

8 They used plant food to _____ the soil.

    a. reduce

    b. extract

    c. enrich

Word Challenge: Example/Not an Example

With a partner or by yourself, think of things that are and are not examples of the words listed below. Write your responses in the chart. The first one has been done for you.

		Example	**Not an Example**
1	**deposit**	You are digging in your yard and you find gold.	You are digging in your yard and you find a tree root.
2	**reduce**		
3	**communicate**		
4	**conserve**		

Word Challenge: What's Your Reason?

Take turns with a partner reading the statements below out loud. Think of a reason for each statement and write it on the line. Write your reasons in complete sentences. The first one has been done for you.

1. It is important to **recycle**. _When we recycle, we use fewer_ _natural resources._

2. We should stop **pollution**. _____

_____

3. Fast-food restaurants should use **reusable** containers. _____

_____

4. Farmers should **enrich** the soil. _____

_____

What's the Answer?

Circle the letter of each correct answer. Some questions may have more than one correct answer. Discuss your choices with a partner.

1 What are some effects of **pollution**?
 a. poor air quality
 b. dirty water
 c. fresh air
 d. snow and rain

2 What is an example of a **deposit**?
 a. a large field
 b. an area with iron ore
 c. a group of lakes
 d. nesting area for birds

3 How can people **conserve** resources?
 a. use less gasoline
 b. use more water
 c. recycle
 d. use more reusable containers

4 How can people **enrich** the earth?
 a. mine it for minerals
 b. put nutrients back into the soil
 c. cut down trees
 d. conserve fuel

Word Study: The Suffixes -er and -or

When a suffix -er or -or is added to a word such as *deposit,* it changes its meaning. The new word names a person or thing that does a job or action.

deposit (v.) to put something somewhere, or to leave something behind
depositor (n.) a person or animal that puts something somewhere or leaves something behind

Add the -er or -or suffix to make new words. Write a definition for each new word. Use a dictionary to check your spelling and your definitions.

	+ -er or -or	Meaning
1 extract		
2 pollute		
3 recycle		
4 communicate		

The Language of Testing

How would you answer a question like this on a test?

What does **the diagram illustrate**?

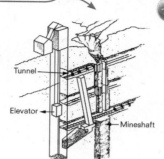

A. a mine
B. erosion
C. the inside of a building
D. how to build a machine

Tunnel

Elevator

Mineshaft

💡 **Tip**

When a question asks you what something *illustrates*, you need to look at a picture to find the answer to the question.

Test Strategy: If you see a question that asks you what something illustrates, rewrite it to ask what the diagram, chart, table or graph shows.

1 How could you say the question above in a different way?

_____

_____

Try the strategy again by asking these questions in a different way.

2 What is illustrated by the diagram?

A. a frog
B. a frog's internal organs
C. a tadpole
D. a toad

_____

_____

_____

3 Which diagram illustrates how aluminum is recycled?

A. 1   C. 3
B. 2   D. 4

_____

_____

_____

In Your Vocabulary Journal

Find each of these words in your Science Vocabulary Journal. Working by yourself or with a partner, use the definitions from pages 62 and 63 of your Work Text to complete the rest of the entry for each word.

communicate	conserve	deposits	enrich	extract
pollution	purpose	recycle	reduce	reusable

Read the passage below. Think about the meanings of the new words printed in **bold**. Underline any words and phrases that contrast a word you know with a new word or idea. The first one has been done for you.

A Tiny Atom

Vocabulary Strategy

Use contrasts to help you understand the meanings of new words. Look for clues that point out contrasts, such as *unlike*, *instead*, or *different from*.

Matter, or everything that you can see or touch, is made of tiny pieces. These bits are called **atoms**. You can think of atoms like grains of sand that make up a beach. A grain of sand, however, is also matter and can be broken into smaller parts. <u>Unlike a grain of sand, an atom is the smallest piece that matter can be broken into.</u> A human hair, for example, is over a million atoms wide! Yet atoms are made up of parts that are even smaller.

Tiny things called protons and neutrons make up most of an atom's **mass**. Mass is how much matter something has inside of it. Protons and neutrons are the center, or nucleus, of the atom. The nucleus of the atom has **density**. It is heavy for being so small. If an atom were about two miles wide, the nucleus would be about the size of a ping-pong ball. Unlike the nucleus of the atom, however, the outer part of the atom has little density. More tiny things called electrons whirl around in this space.

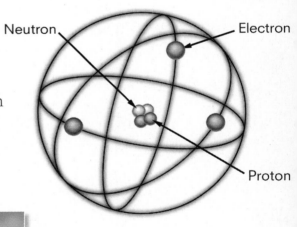

New Science Words

atom
  noun   the smallest part of an element

density
  noun   how thick something is, or how much it weighs compared to its size

mass
  noun   how much matter something has inside it

matter
  noun   anything that takes up space and has weight

Now read this passage and practice the vocabulary strategy again. Underline any words and phrases that contrast something you know with a new word or idea. Look for clues like *unlike*, *instead*, or *different from*.

Drink It, Breathe It, Walk on It

All matter comes in three states or forms. Those three states are **solid**, **liquid**, and **gas**. The atoms in a solid, like a rock, are usually closer together than the atoms of a liquid or a gas. Unlike the atoms in a solid, the atoms in a liquid like water are farther apart. The atoms in a gas, like oxygen, are even farther apart.

Each state of matter also has **volume**. In other words, it takes up space. Usually the solid state of matter has the least volume. In **general**, a liquid has greater volume. One specific liquid, water, is a little different, though. Instead of growing smaller when it freezes into ice, its solid form, it expands, or grows. That's why ice floats in a glass of water. Unlike both a solid and a liquid, a gas can expand to fill any size space. Its atoms have no certain **order** in their movements, so a gas has no shape. That's why there are so many gases in the air we breathe.

More New Science Words

gas
  noun   something that is neither a liquid nor a solid, such as steam

liquid
  noun   something that is neither a gas nor a solid, such as milk

solid
  noun   something that is neither a gas nor a liquid, such as a penny

volume
  noun   the amount of space an object takes up or can hold, or how loud or soft a sound is

Other Useful Words

general
  adjective   not specific

order
  noun   the way things are placed
  verb   to place things in a certain way

Use the Strategy

Look at a chapter in your textbook that your teacher identifies. Use contrasts in the text to help you figure out the meaning of any new words you find. Keep track of these in a chart.

Finish the Sentence

Choose a word to finish each sentence. Write the correct word on the line. Discuss your choices with a partner.

1 The water we drink is a _____.

    gas   **solid**   **liquid**   **ice**

2 All _____ in the universe has weight.

    volume   **density**   **matter**   **atom**

3 Something in its _____ state has a shape.

    solid   **gas**   **liquid**   **atomic**

4 A gas will grow to fill the _____ of any space.

    atom   **matter**   **volume**   **solid**

5 A _____ weighs less than a liquid.

    atom   **gas**   **solid**   **volume**

6 An _____ is very small.

    mass   **volume**   **solid**   **atom**

7 The teacher had us line up in _____ from shortest to tallest.

    order   **atom**   **volume**   **solid**

8 A _____ store sells a lot of different things.

    mass   **liquid**   **general**   **volume**

Word Challenge: Which Word?

With a partner, take turns saying the words listed below. Together, think of a statement for each one that gives a strong clue about its meaning. Write your statement next to the word. The first one has been done for you.

1 **atom** *"I am the smallest part of something."*

2 **solid** _____

3 **volume** _____

4 **gas** _____

Word Challenge: Correct or Incorrect

Read the sentences below with a partner. Decide if the new words in the lesson are used correctly or incorrectly. Write **C** if the sentence is correct. Write **I** if the sentence is incorrect. Rewrite the incorrect sentences. The first one has been done for you.

1 __I__ There are eight states of **matter**.

   There are three states of matter.

2 _____ The **mass** of an object measures how much space it fills.

   _____

3 _____ The ocean is filled with a salty **liquid**.

   _____

4 _____ Her interests are so **general** that she has very few hobbies.

   _____

Analogies

Use a word from the box to finish each sentence. Write the word on the line. Discuss your answers with a partner.

solid	liquid	atom	general

1. Lava is to liquid as rock is to _____.

2. Beach is to a grain of sand as matter is to _____.

3. Orderly is to messy as specific is to _____.

4. Air is to gas as milk is to _____.

Word Study: The Suffix -ify

When the suffix *-ify* is added to a noun such as *gas*, it does two things:
- First, it makes the noun a verb: *gasify*.
- Second, it changes the word's meaning. The word now means "to turn something into gas."

> **Liquid** is a little different. Drop the *-d* from the end of *liquid* before adding *-efy*.
>
> **liquid** (n.) something that is neither a gas nor a solid, such as milk
> **liquefy** (v.) to turn something into liquid

A. Add the *-ify* or *-efy* suffix to make a new word.

	+ *-ify*
1. solid	
2. liquid	
3. gas	

B. Fill each blank with a word from the chart.

We did a great experiment last week. We changed the state of water. First we

put water in the freezer. After two hours, the water became solid ice. We had learned

to _____ water! Then our teacher heated the water until it became

steam. We had learned how to _____ water! Last we let ice melt in a

pan. The ice changed from solid to liquid. We had learned to _____ ice!

The Language of Testing

How would you answer a question like this on a test?

Choose the (best) answer. What is the measure of the amount of matter in a substance?

    A. mass
    B. weight
    C. volume
    D. density

 Tip

When *best* is used in the directions, it means *most correct*. More than one answer might be slightly correct, but only one answer is the most correct or best.

Test Strategy: If you see a question asking for the best answer, rewrite it using the phrase *most correct*.

1 How could you say the question above in a different way?

_____

_____

Try the strategy again by asking these questions in a different way.

2 What are three states of matter?

    A. density, mass, and volume
    B. solid, liquid, gas
    C. solid, liquid, mass
    D. solid, mass, volume

_____

_____

_____

3 What two states of matter generally have the greatest volume?

    A. gas and solid
    B. liquid and solid
    C. liquid and gas
    D. all of the above

_____

_____

_____

In Your Vocabulary Journal

Find each of these words in your Science Vocabulary Journal. Working by yourself or with a partner, use the definitions from pages 68 and 69 of your Work Text to complete the rest of the entry for each word.

atom	**density**	**gas**	**general**	**liquid**
mass	**matter**	**order**	**solid**	**volume**

Read the passage below. Think about the meanings of the new words printed in **bold**. Circle any definitions that might help you figure out what these words mean. Draw an arrow from the definition to the word it describes. The first one has been done for you.

Ben Franklin

Vocabulary Strategy

Look for definitions in the text to help you understand the meanings of new words.

Using a simple kite, Ben Franklin showed that lightning is **electricity**, a kind of energy. Franklin's experiments with electricity went far beyond his kite, however. He made **batteries** to create and store electricity. He was also interested in **static**, a buildup of electricity on an object. You know static as the "shock" you sometimes get from a doorknob. Franklin built machines that would create static electricity. Through those machines, he learned about **conduction**, or how electricity moves from place to place.

Franklin also created the lightning rod. A lightning rod is a tall pole with a wire that goes down to the ground. A lightning rod is placed on the roof of a building to prevent lightning from starting fires. When lightning hits the rod, it moves down the wire and hits the ground. Franklin made the first lightning rod in 1750. Today, lightning rods still protect thousands of buildings.

New Science Words

battery

noun an object that uses water and other materials to store electricity

conduction

noun how heat and energy move through something

electricity

noun a form of energy used for lighting, heating, and powering machines

static

noun a build-up of energy on an object

Now read this passage and practice the vocabulary strategy again. Circle any definitions in the passage that help you figure out what the new words in **bold** mean. Draw an arrow from the definition to the word it describes.

Power Up!

There are hundreds of wires in your home. These wires bring electrical **current** to different parts of your house or apartment. Current is the movement of electricity. Electricity travels in a **circuit**, which is a complete path. When a circuit breaks, the flow of electricity stops. That's what happens when you turn off a light switch. A light switch is **designed**, or made, in such a way to break a circuit.

It is hard to imagine what it would be like to live without electricity. It can be used to light our homes, **heat** them with warm air, or even cool them with fans and air conditioners. Electricity runs our radios and computers. Still, with all these good uses, electricity also has the **potential** to be dangerous. It can start fires. It can also shock, or hurt someone badly. Remember to be safe with electricity.

More New Science Words

circuit

   noun   a complete and closed path that electricity can flow through

current

   noun   a steady movement of water, air, or electricity

heat

   noun   warmth or being hot

potential

   noun   something that is possible but isn't yet real

   adjective   possible, but not yet real

When Ben Franklin said there was **electricity** in the air, they told him to "go fly a kite."

Other Useful Words

design

   verb   to plan and make something to look a certain way or to do something specific

figure

   noun   a picture that shows information about something

   verb   to solve a problem

Use the Strategy

Look at a chapter in your textbook that your teacher identifies. Use definitions in the text to help you figure out the meaning of any new words you find.

Matching

Finish the sentences in Group A with words from Group B. Write the letter of the word on the line.

Group A

1. I got a shock from the metal doorknob because of the _____, or build up of energy on it.

2. Cars, flashlights, and some radios get their power from _____.

3. The _____ from the campfire felt good in the chilly evening.

4. We used math to _____ out, or solve the problem.

Group B

A batteries
B. figure
C. static
D. heat

Group A

5. Our project was to _____ a box that would protect an egg from being crushed.

6. The clouds in the sky meant that there was a _____ for rain.

7. Ben Franklin proved that lighting was a form of _____.

8. The electrical _____ moved through the wire.

Group B

E. design
F. electricity
G. current
H. potential

Word Challenge: Finish the Idea

With a partner, take turns reading the incomplete sentences below. Write an ending for each. The first one has been done for you.

1 We knew the **circuit** was broken because ___the lights and the TV turned off.___

2 I like having things that use **batteries** for power because _____

_____

3 My favorite team had a good **potential** to win many games this season because

_____

4 I would like to **design** _____ because _____

_____

Word Challenge: What's Your Answer?

Take turns with a partner reading each question out loud and writing an answer on the line. Answer the questions in complete sentences. The first one has been done for you.

1 What does it mean if something improves **conduction**?

It means that electricity can move through it better.

2 What would you miss if there were no **electricity**? _____

_____

3 When do you like to have **heat**? _____

_____

4 How would you **figure** out a hard problem? _____

_____

Same or Opposite

In each of the groups, circle the two words that mean the same or almost the same as each other. Discuss your choices with a partner.

1   potential   real

        design   possible

3   heat   warmth

        electricity   water

2   battery   path

        circuit   plug

4   power   electricity

        design   general

Word Study: The Suffix -al

When the suffix -al is added to a word such as education, it changes the word's meaning.

- First, it makes the word an adjective: *educational*.
- Second, it adds "connected to" to the word's meaning.

education (n.) learning and teaching
educational (adj.) connected to learning and teaching

A. Add the -al suffix to make a new word. Write your own definitions for each. Use a dictionary to check your spelling and definitions.

	+ -al	Meaning
1 electric		
2 figure		
3 potent (powerful)		

B. Fill each blank with an -al word from the chart.

1 Something that has to do with a drawing or picture is _____

2 If something has the power to do something, it has _____

3 A clock that is powered by electricity is _____

78

The Language of Testing

How would you answer a question like this on a test?

What conclusion can be drawn from the following clues? <u>You plug a lamp in, there is a popping sound, and all the lights go out.</u>

    A. There is an electrical storm.
    B. Lightning has struck the house.
    C. The circuit for the room is broken.
    D. You forgot to pay your electric bill.

 Tip

When *what conclusion can be drawn* is used in the directions, it means *what happened?* or *why did this happen?* You must choose the best possible reason from the choices given.

Test Strategy: If you see *what conclusion can be drawn* in a test question, place the phrases *what happened?* or *why did this happen?* after the event described.

1 How could you say the question above in a different way?

_____

_____

Try the strategy again by asking these questions in a different way.

2 What conclusion can be drawn from the following event? A flashlight battery works for a short time, but it is dim. Then it goes out.

    A. The lightbulb has gone bad.
    B. You need a new flashlight.
    C. The battery is weak.
    D. The flashlight wasn't made well.

_____

_____

_____

3 An electrician discovers that two wires are not connected. What conclusion can be drawn from this information?

    A. The circuit is not working.
    B. The electrician made a mistake.
    C. The wiring needs to be checked.
    D. All of the above.

_____

_____

_____

In Your Vocabulary Journal

Find each of these words in your Science Vocabulary Journal. Working by yourself or with a partner, use the definitions from pages 74 and 75 of your Work Text to complete the rest of the entry for each word.

battery	circuit	conduction	current	design
electricity	figure	heat	potential	static

Lesson 14
Forces and Motion

Read the passage below. Think about the meanings of the new words printed in **bold**. Underline any examples or descriptions you find that might help you figure out what these words mean. The first one has been done for you.

Isaac Newton

Vocabulary Strategy

Use examples and descriptions to help you figure out the meanings of new words. Look for clues like *for example*, *like*, or *such as*. Look for pictures that show what a new word means, too.

Isaac Newton was one of the greatest scientists of all time. He discovered **gravity**. He figured out that Earth's gravity pulls harder on larger objects than smaller ones. That's why a small stone weighs less than a large one. Gravity was just one **force** that Newton described. <u>An example of a force would be a push or a pull</u>.

Newton also described how forces work with **motion**. An example of this would be how a wagon moves. He said that unless a force is **applied**, or used with something, it will not move. He also said that once an object was in motion, it would stay in motion until something stopped it. Usually **friction** causes an object to stop moving, like the brakes on a car.

In high school you may take a math course called calculus. You can blame Newton for that. He created it!

New Science Words

force
noun something that moves or changes something

friction
noun something that stops one object from moving against another

gravity
noun what causes things to fall toward the ground when dropped

motion
noun movement
verb to make a movement

80

Now read this passage and practice the vocabulary strategy again. Underline the examples and descriptions in the passage. Draw an arrow from each to the word it describes.

Sailors Long Ago

How did sailors long ago figure out the **position** of their boat in the ocean? For example, they could have been a few miles east of Florida. How did they know? Also, how did they know which direction they were heading in?

Before tools were invented to help them, sailors used the stars. Then about a thousand years ago, Chinese sailors began using **magnets** to find direction. You might know that a magnet can pick up pieces of metal. The **poles**, or opposite ends of the magnet, line up with the North Pole, too. This is how a magnet can help you find your direction.

Sailors need to know their position and the direction they are going in so that they can give **instructions** to their crew to avoid dangers in the water. These instructions might be "head south!" or "watch out for the rocks!" If a ship hits rock or sand, it has to be moved into deeper waters. Sailors use ropes and **levers** that look like big see-saws to pull and push the ship back into the water.

More New Science Words

lever
 noun   a bar used to lift a heavy object

magnet
 noun   a piece of metal that can attract some types of metal

poles
 noun   the opposite, or positive and negative, ends of a magnet

position
 noun   place or location

"I think our **exact** position is at the North **Pole**, sir."

Other Useful Words

apply
 verb   to use what you know

instructions
 noun   information that explains how to do something

Use the Strategy

Look at a chapter in your textbook that your teacher identifies. Use examples, descriptions, and pictures in the text to help you figure out the meaning of any new words you find.

Finish the Paragraph

Use the words in **bold** to finish the paragraph below. Write the correct word in the blank. One word will not be used. Discuss your choices with a partner.

force   friction   gravity   magnets   motion   pole   position

Scientists have designed a train that floats above its tracks. It looks like it is not

affected by _____. The trains and tracks have very powerful
1

_____ that hold the train in _____ about four
2   **3**

inches above the track. When the trains are in _____, they can
4

travel at speeds over 300 miles per hour! The trains float above the tracks, so there isn't

_____ from wheels rubbing against the rails. Because of this, it
5

takes very little _____ to move these trains. Full-sized trains are
6

being used in some countries. Someday

you might ride on one of these fast

magnetic trains.

Word Challenge: True or False

Take turns with a partner reading the sentences below out loud. Write **T** next to each sentence that is true. Write **F** next to each sentence that is false. Rewrite the false sentences. The first one has been done for you.

1 ___T___ A **force** is something that pushes or pulls something else.

2 _____ If you had to move a large rock, you would not need a **lever**.

_____

3 _____ **Gravity** causes objects to float off into space.

_____

4 _____ When you **apply** your knowledge to solve a problem, you don't use anything

you have learned.

_____

Word Challenge: Which Word?

With a partner, take turns saying the words listed below. Together, think of a statement for each one that gives a strong clue about its meaning. Write your statement next to the word. The first one has been done for you.

1 **friction** _"I can stop a train in its tracks!"_____

2 **position** _____

3 **pole** _____

4 **instructions** _____

Extend the Meaning

Write the letter of the word or phrase that best completes each sentence. Discuss your choices with a partner.

1 You can find your **position** by _____.
   a. looking at the ground
   b. using a compass
   c. looking behind you

2 You can test a **magnet** by _____.
   a. touching it to iron or steel
   b. its shape
   c. finding its poles

3 You might use a **lever** to _____.
   a. dig a hole
   b. build a bridge
   c. help move a stuck car

4 The **poles** of a magnet are _____.
   a. always flat
   b. opposites
   c. always labeled

Word Study: The Suffix -ation and -tion

When the suffix –*ation* or -*tion* is added to a verb such as *locate*, two things happen:
 • First, it makes the word a noun: *location*.
 • Second, it changes the word's meaning. The word now means "the place where something is."

locate (v.) to find or to place something
location (n.) the place where something is

A. Add the suffix -*ation* or -*tion* to make a new word. Use a dictionary to check your spelling.

		Definition	+ -*ation* or -*tion*
1	**gravitate**	to move toward something	
2	**posit**	to place something somewhere	
3	**apply**	to use what you know	

B. Write a new -*ation* or -*tion* word in each blank.

1 I posited the book on the shelf so I will know its _____ when I need to find it.

2 Myra wanted to apply for a job, so she asked for an _____.

3 Dead leaves gravitate to the ground. I think it's because of Earth's _____.

84

The Language of Testing

How would you answer a question like this on a test?

What is the (**major cause**) of heat in the brakes of a car?

A. the car's speed
B. friction
C the heat of the roadway
D. the outside air temperature

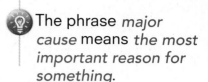

The phrase *major cause* means *the most important reason for something.*

Test Strategy: If the question has the phrase *major cause* in it, restate the question using *most important reason for*. You can also add the phrase *is a major cause of . . .* to each answer choice to see if it is right or wrong.

1 What phrase would you use to test each answer choice above?

_____

_____

Try the strategy again by adding a test phrase to the answer choices below. Write your test phrase below each question.

2 What is a major cause of earthquakes?

a. the shifting of the earth's crust
b. volcanic eruptions
c. ocean tides
d. underground explosions

_____

_____

_____

3 Choose a major cause of electrical fires.

a. too many electrical lines
b. faulty wiring
c. lightning
d. bad fuses

_____

_____

_____

In Your Vocabulary Journal

Find each of these words in your Science Vocabulary Journal. Working by yourself or with a partner, use the definitions from pages 80 and 81 of your Work Text to complete the rest of the entry for each word.

apply	**force**	**friction**	**gravity**	**instructions**
lever	**magnet**	**motion**	**pole**	**position**

Lesson 15 Sound and Light

Read the passage below. Think about the meanings of the new words printed in **bold**. Create connections between the new words and words you know. These will help you remember what the new words mean. Mark or write these connections near the new words in the passage. The first one has been done for you.

A Trick of the Light?

Vocabulary Strategy

Create connections between new words and words you know. You can use a Word Anchor chart to help you create connections.

Optics is the study of how light works and how we see. People have been interested in optics for thousands of years. As early as 200 BCE, Greek thinkers studied how mirrors could **reflect** light, bouncing it back in different ways. Legend has it that one person used a mirror to win a battle. He reflected the sun's **rays** into the eyes of the enemy. The bright, narrow flashes of light blinded them.

Early scientists also experimented with **prisms**, which separated light into different colors, like a rainbow.

Around CE 1200, people began to focus light through a **lens**, a thin piece of curved glass. They found that the shape of a lens could make an image look larger or smaller. A thicker lens that curves outwards on both sides makes a larger image. A thinner lens that curves inward on both sides makes a smaller one.

New Science Words

lens
   noun a piece of clear glass or plastic that is curved on one or both sides

prism
   noun a clear piece of glass or plastic that is shaped like a triangle and separates light into colors

ray
   noun a narrow beam of light

reflect
   verb to bounce light, sound, or heat off an object

Now read this passage and practice the vocabulary strategy again. Write near or mark in the text any connections you can use to help you "anchor" the meaning of new words.

Guitar Strings

Do you like to listen to rock music? Most rock bands **include** or have one or more guitar players. The strings of those guitars can teach us something about sound. When a player strums the guitar, the strings start to **vibrate**. As the strings move back and forth very fast, they create sound that we can hear. In fact, this movement is actually **visible** if you look at the string.

The highness or lowness of the sound, or **pitch**, depends on the length of the string. As a guitar player moves his or her fingers up and down the neck of the guitar, the vibrating part of the string gets shorter or longer. The sound from the shorter string is higher. The longer string makes a lower pitch. Guitars are built to make the sound of the strings clear and loud. They use wood and other materials that will not **absorb** the sound like a sponge absorbs water.

More New Science Words

absorb
> *verb* to soak up something

pitch
> *noun* the highness or lowness of a sound

vibrate
> *verb* to move back and forth very quickly

visible
> *adjective* seen by the human eye

Arturo thought that sponges would **absorb** the sound of Kelley's horrible music.

Other Useful Words

include
> *verb* to make one or more things part of something else

prove
> *noun* to show something is true or real

Use the Strategy

Look at a chapter in your textbook that your teacher identifies. Use associations to help you anchor your understanding of any new words you find.

The Right Word

Read each sentence. Look at the word or phrase that is underlined. Write one of the words from the box that means the same or almost the same thing as the underlined part of the sentence. Discuss your answers with a partner.

lenses	prism	rays	reflected

1 _____ They had to replace the <u>curved pieces of glass</u> in my glasses because they were scratched.

2 _____ <u>Narrow beams of light</u> from the afternoon sun came in through the window.

3 _____ The trees on the shore <u>sent back an image</u> off the still water of the lake.

4 _____ The light that came through the <u>clear piece of glass shaped like a triangle</u> made colors on the wall.

absorb	pitch	vibrate	visible

5 _____ We used paper towels to <u>soak up</u> the water that was spilled on the floor.

6 _____ The singer couldn't find the right <u>highness or lowness of sound</u> and sounded horrible.

7 _____ The lights of the city were <u>seen by the human eye</u> from many miles away.

8 _____ We could feel the engine <u>move very quickly back and forth</u> as soon as the old car started.

Word Challenge: Describe the Scene

Take turns with a partner reading each question out loud and writing an answer on the line. Answer the questions in complete sentences. The first one has been done for you.

1 The padding on the walls **absorbed** the sound of the music. How did the

music sound? *The music sounded very quiet and muffled.*

2 The blinds were closed, but a **ray** of sun came through. What did the sunlight

look like? _____

_____

3 The flowers in the backyard were **reflected** in the mirror. What could you see?

_____

4 You want to **prove** to your friends that you know a hard skateboard trick. What do

you do? _____

_____

Word Challenge: Finish the Idea

With a partner, take turns reading the incomplete sentences below. Write an ending for each. The first one has been done for you.

1 The guitar string **vibrated** because *the player plucked it.*

2 The white light went through the **prism** and _____

_____

3 We knew the trumpet was off **pitch** because _____

_____

4 We did not **include** his brother in our game because _____

_____

Categories

Write the words from the word bank in the correct boxes below. Two words may be used in both boxes.

absorb	lens	pitch	prism	ray	reflect	vibrate	visible

Sound Words	Light Words

Word Study: The Root *vis*

The root *vis* means *see*. You can add many prefixes and suffixes to *vis* to make new words.

> **vis** (root) to see
> **visible** (adj.) able to be seen
> **invisible** (adj.) unable to be seen

Add the prefixes and suffixes to *vis* to make new words. Provide definitions for the words you create. Use a dictionary to check your spelling and definitions.

1 *vis + ual =* _____ Means _____

_____

2 *vis + ual+ ize =* _____ Means _____

_____

3 *visible + ity=* _____ Means _____

_____

4 *in + visible + ity=* _____ Means _____

_____

The Language of Testing

How would you answer a question like this on a test?

(What was the result) when the length of
the vibrating string was shortened?

   A. The pitch became lower.
   B. The pitch became higher.
   C. The sound was softer.
   D. The sound was louder.

 Tip

The phrase *what was
the result* can also mean
what happened after.

Test Strategy: If you see a question that uses the phrase *what was the result*, rewrite
it using the phrase *what happened after*.

1 How could you say the question above in a different way?

_____

_____

Try the strategy again by asking these questions in a different way.

2 What was the result when the light
passed through a concave lens?

   A. The image became smaller.
   B. The image became larger.
   C. The light was broken into
      different colors.
   D. The image was reversed.

3 What was the result when layers of
newspaper were wrapped around
the speaker?

   A. The sound was improved.
   B. The low pitches became clearer.
   C. The sound was absorbed.
   D. The high pitches became clearer.

_____

_____

_____

_____

_____

_____

In Your Vocabulary Journal

Find each of these words in your Science Vocabulary Journal. Working by yourself or
with a partner, use the definitions from pages 86 and 87 of your Work Text to complete
the rest of the entry for each word.

absorb	**include**	**lens**	**pitch**	**prism**
prove	**ray**	**reflect**	**vibrate**	**visible**

Glossary

Aa

absorb (uhb **sawrb**)
verb to soak up something (*Thick material can **absorb** sound.*)

adapt (uh **dapt**)
verb to change to fit into a new or different situation (*Some lizards **adapt** to a new place by changing color.*)

amphibian (am **fib** ee uhn)
noun a cold-blooded animal that lives in water when it is young and on land when it is older (*Maddie spends so much time swimming that we call her an **amphibian**.*)

apply (uh **ply**)
verb to use what you know (*He was able to **apply** what he learned and invented a new computer.*)

atmosphere (**at** muhs fir)
noun the layer of air around the earth (*The earth's **atmosphere** is about 300 miles thick.*)

atom (**at** uhm)
noun the smallest part of an element (*Even with a powerful microscope, an **atom** is too small to be seen.*)

axis (**ak** suhs)
noun an imaginary line that runs through the center of something (*The earth spins on its **axis**.*)

Bb

bacteria (bak **tir** ee uh)
noun very tiny living things that can either be helpful or cause disease (*Yasmin washed the kitchen counter to kill the **bacteria**.*)

battery (**ba** tuh ree)
noun an object that uses water and other materials to store electricity (*We had to put a **battery** into the flashlight before it would work.*)

Cc

carbon (**kahr** buhn)
noun a material found in the earth that is neccesary for life (*Coal and diamonds are forms of **carbon**.*)

cause (**kahz**)
verb to make something happen (*The heavy rains **caused** a flood.*)
noun the reason why something happens (*Lightning was the **cause** of the fire.*)

cell (**sel**)
noun the smallest part of all living things (*There are millions of **cells** in the human body.*)

chart (**chahrt**)
noun a drawing that shows information in a way that makes it easy to understand (*Nick made a **chart** showing what he needed to know for the test.*)

circuit (**suhr** kuht)
noun a complete and closed path that electricity can flow through (*The lights went out when the **circuit** was broken.*)

classify (**klas** uh fy)
verb to sort things into groups by how they are alike (*We had to **classify** plants by the shape of their leaves.*)

climate (**kly** muht)
noun the usual weather of a large area (*Southern California has a warm **climate**.*)

communicate (kuh **myoo** nuh kayt)
   verb to share information through
      speaking, writing, or movements
      (*She was able to* **communicate**
      because she spoke their language.)

community (kuh **myu** nuh tee)
   noun a group of plants, animals, or people
      living in the same area (*A* **community**
      of beavers was building a dam.)

compare (**kuhm** pehr)
   verb to look at two things to see how they
      are alike and different (*Jon looked at*
      the two flowers to **compare** *their size,*
      shape, and color.)

conduct (**kuhn** duhkt)
   verb to plan and do something (*The*
      students were asked to **conduct**
      an experiment.)

conduction (**kuhn** duhk shuhn)
   noun how heat and energy move through
      something (*Hot water warms our*
      house through **conduction**.)

conserve (kunh **suhrv**)
   verb to use something carefully so it will
      last longer (*We have to* **conserve** *our*
      water because we don't want the well
      to go dry.)

consume (cuhn **soom**)
   verb to eat, take in, or use up (*Cars and*
      trucks **consume** *a lot of gasoline.*)

continent (**kahn** tuh nuhnt)
   noun one of seven large areas of land on
      Earth (*The seven* **continents** *are*
      Africa, Antarctica, Asia, Australia,
      Europe, North America, and South
      America.)

control (kuhn **trohl**)
   noun something in an experiment that
      everything else is compared to (*The*
      control *in Carla's experiment was*
      dry seeds.)

   verb to have power over something (*Alia*
      used a whistle to **control** *her dog.*)

core (kawr)
   noun the very center part of the earth
      (*How could* **scientists** *dig to the core*
      of the earth?)

crust (kruhst)
   noun the outer layer of the earth
      (*Mountains, fields, and the ocean floor*
      are all part of the earth's **crust**.)

current (**kuhr** uhnt)
   noun a steady movement of water, air, or
      electricity (*The lamp was unplugged,*
      so no **current** *went through the cord.*)

cycle (**sy** kul)
   noun a string of things that happen over
      and over again in the same order
      (*The months and seasons follow the*
      same **cycle** *every year.*)

Dd

decay (di **kay**)
   verb to rot or break down (*The wet leaves*
      on the ground began to **decay**.)

density (**dehn** suh tee)
   noun how thick something is or how much
      something weighs compared to its
      size (*The* **density** *of iron is greater*
      than the density of cork.)

deposit (di **pah** zuhts)
   noun a natural layer of something that
      builds up over time (*There were*
      rich **deposits** *of copper in northern*
      Michigan.)

   verb to place something or leave
      something behind (*We* **deposited**
      all of the money in the bank.)

desert (**dehz** uhrt)
   noun a dry area of land with few plants
      (*The sandy, dry Sahara is the largest*
      desert *in the world.*)

design (di **zyn**)
  verb   to plan and make something to look
         a certain way or to do something
         specific (*He had **designed** the car to
         be the fastest in the world.*)

develop (duh **vehl** uhp)
  verb   to grow or change over a period of
         time (*Jeff ran every day to **develop**
         strong muscles.*)

dinosaur (**dy** nuh sawr)
  noun   a large animal that lived many
         thousands of years ago (*The museum
         had a room full of **dinosaur** bones.*)

divide (duh **vyd**)
  verb   to split into two or more parts (*Cells
         divide when they reproduce.*)

Ee

earthquake (**uhrth** kwayk)
  noun   when the ground shakes because
         the outer layer of the earth is moving
         (*The last **earthquake** in California
         damaged several buildings.*)

ecosystem (**ee** koh **sis** tuhm)
  noun   the plants, animals, and nonliving
         things in an area that have a
         relationship with one another (*The tall
         trees, birds, monkeys, and insects of
         the rain forest share an **ecosystem**.*)

effect (ih **fehkt**)
  noun   a change that happens because of
         something else (*The science project
         studied the **effect** people have on the
         earth.*)

electricity (ih lehk **tri** suh tee)
  noun   a form of energy used for lighting,
         heating, and powering machines
         (*Without **electricity**, I couldn't use my
         computer.*)

embryo (**ehm** bree oh)
  noun   an early part of an animal's life, not
         long before it is born (*We could see
         the tiny fish **embryo** inside of the egg.*)

energy (**ehn** ur jee)
  noun   the power or strength needed to do
         work or grow (*A healthy breakfast
         gives a person **energy** for the day.*)

enrich (in **rich**)
  verb   to make something better by adding
         other things (*Mixing compost with the
         dirt **enriches** the soil.*)

environment (in **vy** ruhn muhnt)
  noun   the natural world of land, sea, and
         air and the things that affect it
         (*We have to be careful to protect
         our **environment**.*)

erosion (ih **roh** zhuhn)
  noun   the wearing away of dirt or rock by
         wind, ice, or water (***Erosion** was
         causing deep ruts near the riverbank.*)

evaporation (ih va puh **ray** shuhn)
  noun   the way in which water seems to
         disappear into the air (*Because of
         evaporation, we had to water the
         plants daily.*)

examine (ig **zam** uhn)
  verb   to look at or check something very
         carefully (*The doctor used a light to
         help her **examine** the back of my
         throat.*)

example (ig **zam** puhl)
  noun   something that can stand for a certain
         group (*One **example** of an evergreen
         tree is the common pine.*)

experiment (ik **spehr** uh mehnt)
  noun   a scientific test that is done to prove
         something or to find how one
         thing affects another (*Lin did an
         experiment to show that salt water
         boils faster than fresh water.*)

explore (ik **splawr**)
  verb   to learn about something unfamiliar,
         or to travel through an unknown area
         to learn about it (*Someday people
         hope to **explore** Mars.*)

extract (ik **strakt**)

    verb   to take something out of something else (*The miners learned how to* **extract** *gold from the rocks.*)

Ff

figure (**fi** gyuhr)

    noun   a picture that shows information about something (*Look at the switch shown in* **figure** *3.*)

figure (out)

    verb   to solve a problem (*We had to use math to* **figure out** *the puzzle.*)

force (**fawrs**)

    noun   something that moves or changes something (*The* **force** *of the wind knocked the tree over.*)

forest (**fawr** ist)

    noun   a large area of land where many trees grow close together (*I like to walk in* **forests** *that have very old and tall trees.*)

form (**fawrm**)

    verb   to make something (*Ice began to* **form** *on the top of the water.*)

fossil (**fah** suhl)

    noun   the parts of dead plants or animals that have turned into rock (**Fossils** *of plants can be found all over the world.*)

friction (**frik** shuhn)

    noun   something that stops one object from moving against another (**Friction** *in the door hinge makes it squeak.*)

front (**fruhnt**)

    noun   the edge of a mass of warm or cold air (*It snowed after the cold* **front** *passed through.*)

fungus (**fuhn** guhs)

    noun   a living thing that is like a plant but has no roots, leaves, or flowers (**Fungus** *was growing on the tree.*)

Gg

gas (**gas**)

    noun   something that is neither a liquid nor a solid, such as steam (*Oxygen is a* **gas** *in the air we breathe.*)

general (**gehn** ruhl)

    adjective   not specific (*She had a* **general** *knowledge of science but wasn't an expert.*)

glacier (**glay** shuhr)

    noun   a huge, slowly moving sheet of ice (*Many* **glaciers** *are found high in the mountains.*)

grain (**grayn**)

    noun   a small, hard seed that is often eaten for food or a small piece of something, like sand (*Most breakfast cereals are made from* **grains** *such as corn, oats, and wheat.*)

graph (**graf**)

    noun   a kind of drawing that compares numbers or amounts using lines, bars, or parts of a circle (*The* **graph** *showed the number of students in each science class.*)

gravity (**gra** vuh tee)

    noun   what causes things to fall toward the ground when dropped (*Without* **gravity** *everything would float away.*)

Hh

habitat (**ha** buh tat)

    noun   the natural place where a plant or animal lives and grows (*The ocean is a* **habitat** *where fish, dolphins, and other creatures live.*)

hatch (**hach**)

    verb   to come out of an egg (*At the farm, we saw baby chicks* **hatch** *from their eggs.*)

heat (**heet**)

noun   warmth or being hot (*We could feel the **heat** coming from the campfire.*)

humidity (hyoo **mi** duh tee)

noun   the amount of wetness in the air (*Before it rained, the **humidity** was very high.*)

hypothesis (hy **pahth** uh sis)

noun   a guess or an idea that can be tested (*Maya proved her **hypothesis** that plants need water and light.*)

Ii

identify (**eye** dehn tih fy)

verb   to name or point out a certain person, animal, or thing (*Sara's grandmother can **identify** many birds just by their calls.*)

include (in **klood**)

verb   to make one or more things part of something else (*The teacher told us to **include** lots of facts in our report.*)

instructions (in **struhk** shuhns)

noun   information that explains how to do something (*I followed the **instructions** and circled the answers.*)

Ll

label (**lay** buhl)

verb   to place a name on something (*They had to **label** the pictures of different types of climates.*)

lava (**lah** vuh)

noun   hot, melted rock (*The **lava** flowed down the side of the mountain.*)

law (**lahw**)

noun   a rule that says that things should always happen in a certain way (*Newton's **laws** explain motion.*)

leaf (**leef**)

noun   part of a plant that is flat, thin, and usually green (*The large, green **leaf** turned red in the fall.*)

lens (**lehnz**)

noun   a piece of clear glass or plastic that is curved on one of both sides (*The **lens** on a magnifying glass curves outward on both sides.*)

lever (**leh** vuhr)

noun   a bar used to lift a heavy object (*We used a **lever** to pry the large rock out of the ground.*)

liquid (**li** kwuhd)

noun   something that is neither a gas nor a solid, such as milk (*You can pour the **liquid** into that bowl.*)

lunar (**loo** nuhr)

adjective   having to do with the moon (*The spacecraft made a **lunar** landing.*)

Mm

magnet (**mag** nuht)

noun   a piece of metal that can attract some other types of metal (*The **magnet** was so strong that it could pick up a car!*)

mammal (**ma** muhl)

noun   a warm-blooded animal that feeds its babies milk (*A doctor that treats **mammals** has to know how they have babies.*)

mantle (**man** tuhl)

noun   the layer of the earth between the center and the outer crust (*The earth's **mantle** is almost 2,000 miles thick.*)

mass (**mas**)

noun   how much matter something has inside it (*The **mass** of the metal cube was 28 grams.*)

matter (**ma** tuhr)

noun   anything that takes up space and has weight (*Solids, liquids, and gasses are the three forms of **matter**.*)

measure (**mehzh** uhr)

verb to figure out the size of an object or how far two places are from each other (*Some scientists **measure** the distance between stars.*)

method (**mehth** uhd)

noun a certain way of doing something (*My brother has an interesting **method** for loading the dishwasher.*)

mineral (**min** ruhl)

noun a nonliving material found in nature such as salt, iron, and silver (*Some **minerals**, such as gold, are worth a lot of money.*)

model (**mahd** uhl)

noun a copy of something that shows its details, how it works, or what it is made of (*The teacher held up a large **model** of a small insect.*)

verb to show how to do something (*The teacher will **model** how to make a graph.*)

motion (**moh** shuhn)

noun movement (*Looking out the window, we could see the train was in **motion**.*)

verb to make a movement (*Dad **motioned** for us to come inside.*)

Nn

nitrogen (**ny** truh juhn)

noun a colorless material found in nature in the air and in the soil (***Nitrogen** in the ground is a nutrient for most plants.*)

notice (**noh** tuhs)

verb to see or to become aware of something (*Jorge didn't **notice** that the plant needed water.*)

nucleus (**noo** klee uhs)

noun the central part of a cell (*The **nucleus** tells all the parts of a cell what to do.*)

nutrients (**noo** tree uhnts)

noun something plants and animals need to stay strong and healthy (*You can get many **nutrients** from fruits and vegetables.*)

Oo

orbit (**awr** buht)

noun the curved path an object makes around a larger object in space (*The earth makes an **orbit** around the sun once a year.*)

verb to travel in a curved path around a large object (*The moon **orbits** the earth about every 28 days.*)

order (**awr** duhr)

noun the way things are placed (*The words in a dictionary are in alphabetical **order**.*)

verb to place things in a certain way (*Our classrooms are **ordered** by age.*)

ovary (**oh** vuh ree)

noun the part of a female animal's body that makes eggs (*Male animals do not have **ovaries** so they cannot make eggs.*)

oxygen (**ahk** si juhn)

noun a colorless material in the air that is needed by most life (*The climber carried a small tank of **oxygen** to help her breathe in the thin air.*)

Pp

phase (**fayz**)

noun a stage in the way the moon looks from Earth (*Last night, the moon was in its full **phase**.*)

photosynthesis (**foh** toh **sin** thuh suhs)

    noun how green plants make food from sunlight, water, and air (*During* **photosynthesis**, *plants give off oxygen, which people need to breathe.*)

pitch (**pich**)

    noun the highness or lowness of a sound (*Her voice had a very high* **pitch**.)

planet (**pla** nuht)

    noun a large rock, such as Earth, that moves around a star (*Besides Earth, eight other* **planets** *circle our sun.*)

poles (**pohlz**)

    noun the opposite ends of a magnet (*The positive* **pole** *of a magnet is attracted to the negative pole.*)

pollution (puh **loo** shuhn)

    noun something that dirties and harms the water, soil, and air (*There was so much* **pollution** *in the air that people had to stay inside.*)

population (**pahp** yuh **lay** shuhn)

    noun the number of plants, animals, or humans that live in a certain area (*The* **population** *of our town grew as people moved here to find jobs.*)

position (puh **zi** shuhn)

    noun place or location (*The guide pointed to our* **position** *on the map.*)

potential (puh **tehn** shuhl)

    noun something that is possible but isn't yet real (*The dry forest meant there could be a* **potential** *forest fire.*)

    adjective possible, but not yet real (*I was a* **potential** *choice for the lead in the school play.*)

predict (pri **dikt**)

    verb to say what will happen (*A meteorologist is a scientist who studies and* **predicts** *the weather.*)

pressure (**presh** uhr)

    noun the effect of one thing pushing on another (*A change in air* **pressure** *usually means a change of weather.*)

prism (**pri** zuhm)

    noun a clear piece of glass or plastic that is shaped like a triangle and separates light into colors (*The light through the* **prism** *made rainbow colors on the wall.*)

produce (pruh **doos**)

    verb to make something or to make something happen (*Bees* **produce** *honey.*)

prove (**proov**)

    noun to show something is true or real (*We had to* **prove** *that our experiment worked.*)

purpose (**puhr** puhs)

    noun the reason for doing something (*The* **purpose** *of today's class was to prepare for the test.*)

Rr

ray (**ray**)

    noun a narrow beam of light (*A* **ray** *of sunlight came through the window.*)

recognize (**reh** kig nayz)

    verb to know what something is because of its features (*Mrs. Gonzales* **recognized** *the difference between the two pieces of metal.*)

record (ri **kawrd**)

    verb to put information in writing (*They were asked to* **record** *what they learned from their experiment.*)

record (**reh** kuhrd)

    noun information that has been saved (*A page in Ana's journal was a* **record** *of her tour of a copper mine.*)

recycle (ree **sy** kuhl)

verb   to use something over again, sometimes in a different way (*We* **recycle** *all our soda cans so the metal can be used again.*)

reduce (ri **doos**)

verb   to make the amount of something less or smaller (*There are many ways to* **reduce** *the amount of electricity you use.*)

reflect (ri **flehkt**)

verb   to bounce light, sound, or heat off an object (*The moonlight was* **reflected** *on the pond.*)

relationship (ree **lay** shuhn ship)

noun   how one thing connects to or affects another (*What is a* **relationship** *between a spilled glass of milk and a happy cat?*)

reproduce (ree pruh **doos**)

verb   to make a copy of something or to produce young (*Some animals* **reproduce** *by laying eggs.*)

reptile (**rehp** tyl)

noun   a cold-blooded animal lays eggs and is often covered with scales (*Some people think that* **reptiles** *are mean because they have cold blood.*)

results (ri **zuhlts**)

noun   what is discovered or learned from an experiment (*The* **results** *showed that some plants grow faster than others.*)

reusable (ree **yooz** uh buhl)

adjective   can be used more than one time (*I bring my meal in* **reusable** *lunch bags.*)

revolve (ri **vahlv**)

verb   to turn in a circle around a center (*The earth* **revolves** *once every 24 hours.*)

role (**rohl**)

noun   the job that someone or something has to do (*A policeman's* **role** *is to keep people safe.*)

root (**root**)

noun   the part of a plant that grows under the ground (*The small pine tree's* **roots** *grew deep in the soil.*)

Ss

satellite (**sa** tuhl ayt)

noun   an object that moves around larger object in space, like a planet (*Photos from the* **satellite** *showed parts of North America.*)

scientist (**sy** un tist)

noun   a person who is an expert in science (*Jenny's mother is a* **scientist** *who studies the weather.*)

sediment (**seh** duh muhnt)

noun   sand and dirt at the bottom of a river or lake or what is left behind by moving water (*The water wasn't clear because of all the* **sediment** *in the lake.*)

seedling (**seed** ling)

noun   a young plant that has its first leaves (*Very young* **seedlings** *might have leaves that are curled.*)

simple (**sim** puhl)

adjective   having few parts or details (*Some* **simple** *plants just have one cell.*)

solar (**sohl** uhr)

adjective   having to do with the sun (*Some people use* **solar** *power to make electricity.*)

solid (**sah** luhd)

noun   something that is neither a gas nor a liquid, such as a penny (*When a liquid like water freezes, it becomes a* **solid**.)

species (**spee** sees)

noun   a group of plants or animals that are alike in important ways (*Dogs and cats are different* **species**.)

sprout (sprowt)

    verb   to grow from a seed (*The seeds we planted have begun to* **sprout**.)

    noun   a very young plant just coming out of its seed (*Young* **sprouts** *need to be protected until they grow taller and stronger.*)

static (sta tik)

    noun   a build-up of energy on an object (*I got a shock from the electrical* **static** *when I touched the brass doorknob.*)

stem (stehm)

    noun   the thin, upright part of a plant above ground (*The yellow flower was at the top of the plant's* **stem**.)

surface (suhr fuhs)

    noun   the top or outside layer of something (*The* **surface** *of the rock was very smooth.*)

Tt

temperature (tehm puh chuhr)

    noun   the amount of warmth in something (*The* **temperature** *today will reach almost 90 degrees.*)

theory (thee uh ree)

    noun   a statement, based on facts, that explains why or how something happens (*Albert Einstein came up with the* **theory** *of relativity.*)

thermometer (thuhr mah muh tuhr)

    noun   a tool for measuring how warm something is (*The* **thermometer** *showed that it was below freezing.*)

tropical (trahp ih kuhl)

    adjective   having to do with the tropics, a very hot and wet part of the earth (*Some people who live in cold places like to visit* **tropical** *areas.*)

Vv

vertebrate (vur tuh brayt)

    noun   a kind of animal that has a backbone (**Vertebrates** *do not need shells because they have backbones.*)

vibrate (vy brayt)

    verb   to move back and forth very quickly (*You can hear the sound of a violin when the strings* **vibrate**.)

visible (vi zuh buhl)

    adjective   seen by the human eye (*The bright light made the colors of the cave wall more* **visible**.)

volcano (vahl kay noh)

    noun   a mountain that sometimes explodes, letting melted rock, ash, and gas come out of the earth (*Many people feared that lava from the* **volcano** *would destroy the town.*)

volume (vahl yoom)

    noun   the amount of space an object takes up or can hold, or how loud or soft a sound is (*The box had a* **volume** *of one cubic foot.*)